LOCOMOTION PAPERS

G000243465

The
Ely Valley Railway
Llantrisant-Penygraig

by
Colin Chapman

THE OAKWOOD PRESS

© Oakwood Press & Colin Chapman 2000

British Library Cataloguing in Publication Data
A Record for this book is available from the British Library
ISBN 0 85361 558 6

Typeset by Oakwood Graphics.
Repro by Ford Graphics, Ringwood, Hants.
Printed by Oakdale Printing Co. Ltd, Poole, Dorset.

Above: An unidentified class '56XX' 0-6-2T brings a coal train bound for Barry Docks off the Ely Valley line at Llantrisant on 14th July, 1960. *Robert Darlaston*

Title page: A general view of Cambrian Colliery, Clydach Vale, with a GWR 0-6-0ST and brake van, *c.* 1910. *J.A. Peden*

Front cover: An up goods train from Penygraig to Llantrisant near the site of Dinas Isha signal box in the summer of 1962. The presence of cattle trucks in such a train at this late date is noteworthy. *Graham Croad Collection*

Rear cover: '14XX' class 0-4-2T No. 1471 stands in the bay platform at Llantrisant station with an afternoon train to Penygraig in June 1958. *D. Chaplin*

Published by The Oakwood Press (Usk), P.O. Box 13, Usk, Mon., NP15 1YS.
E-mail: oakwood-press@dial.pipex.com
Website: www.oakwood-press.dial.pipex.com

Contents

'14XX' class 0-4-2T No. 1471 with a Diagram A9 matchboard-sided auto-trailer (converted from a steam railcar) and crew in the Penygraig bay at Llantrisant in September 1954.
D. Chaplin

Preface

Until the end of November 1951 Llantrisant, midway between Cardiff and Bridgend on the South Wales main line, acted as junction station for three branch line passenger services. To the casual observer each of these appeared to be typically ex-Great Western Railway with that company's characteristic auto-trains or, in the case of the Cowbridge line, one of its distinctive diesel railcars, connecting with the main line stopping trains. However, beneath this superficial gloss each branch had its own distinctive character and background. Two had been part of the Taff Vale Railway (TVR) until 1922: that to the south of the station had been built by the Cowbridge Railway, an impecunious rural concern promoted by local interests, initially with TVR support; while trains from Llantrisant ran to Pontypridd over the metals of the Llantrissant and Taff Vale Junction Railway (L&TVJR), a nominally independent offshoot of the TVR intended to tap the iron ore and coal produce of the area.

The third branch - the Ely Valley line - appeared to be the most modern, with double track and stations dating from around the turn of the century. Appearances were deceptive, however, as this was, in fact, the oldest of the three branches, having been opened in 1860 as a single track, broad gauge mineral line by the Ely Valley Railway Company (EVR). Extensively modernised in connection with the doubling of the line and the subsequent introduction of passenger trains, it remained an independent concern (although leased by the GWR) until amalgamation with the larger company in 1902.

From 1951 the branches radiating from Llantrisant were progressively stripped away. First to go was that to Cowbridge, closed in November of that year, followed by the Pontypridd service in March 1952. The Ely Valley line passenger trains clung on until 1958, their departure leaving Llantrisant with only the main line stopping service. Closed in 1964, the station was reborn in 1992 with the geographically more correct but to the railway historian rather prosaic title of 'Pontyclun'.

This book completes the author's trilogy of studies of the network of branch lines centred on Llantrisant station, and follows on from the earlier histories of the Cowbridge Railway and the L&TVJR. Apart from the South Wales main line and its associated facilities little of railway interest now remains in the area, but hopefully the memories will live on.

Place Names

The spelling of place names can often be a cause of confusion when dealing with the railway history of South Wales. Modern spellings are used throughout this work, except in the case of certain railway companies where the 'statutory' titles are used.

The names of branches can also change, again giving rise to confusion. The Mwyndy branch, so-called by the EVR, was later referred to as the 'Brofiscin branch'; likewise the Gellyrhaidd branch became known as the 'Hendreforgan branch' in GWR days. In the hope of avoiding such difficulties the EVR names are used throughout.

Chapter One

Background and Early Schemes

Of the three rivers that flow to the Bristol Channel at and near Cardiff - the Ely, the Taff and the Rhymney - the Ely is perhaps the least well-known. Nevertheless, its valley has its own unique character, differing in many ways from that of its nearest neighbour, the Taff. Upstream of the extensive mudflats and moors, found near its mouth, the Ely flows through rolling countryside forming a prosperous agricultural district. It is only above its halfway point, near the town of Llantrisant, that the valley of the Ely takes on much of the character typical of the South Wales coalfield, steep-sided as a result of glaciation, but with gaps and side valleys providing potential routes to the adjoining Ogmore and Rhondda river systems. In pre-glacial times the two Rhondda rivers had formed the headwaters of the River Ely, but had later been captured by an aggressive tributary of the River Taff striking westwards from what is now Pontypridd. This had left behind two gaps in the hills at the head of the Ely Valley, at Penygraig and Trebanog. The more important of the two was that at Penygraig, opening up the prospect of a direct but somewhat elevated route from the Ely Valley into that of the Rhondda Fawr.

A brief digression on the geology of the area may be helpful at this point. The South Wales coalfield takes the form of a basin with the coal and associated measures rising gently to become exposed in the so-called 'Northern Crop' at Merthyr and the Heads of the Valleys. Its southern counterpart, on the other hand, rises much more steeply to form the line of hills stretching from south-east of Caerphilly to Kenfig Hill, to the west of Bridgend. The River Taff breaks through this ridge in dramatic fashion at Taffs Well, while the River Ely is a little more restrained at Llantrisant. Running east-west across the centre of the coalfield basin is an upward fold in the strata - the Pontypridd Anticline - which results in the lower coal measures being brought nearer the surface than otherwise would be the case. This important feature was not fully appreciated in the early years of the exploitation of the coal reserves of the Rhondda and adjoining valleys, it being thought that only the upper household and coking coal measures could be worked economically in this part of the coalfield.

To the south-east of Llantrisant, in a belt of carboniferous limestone, were to be found deposits of haematite iron ore. This source had been worked since Roman times, but it was not until the middle of the 19th century that its exploitation took place on a significant scale.

The pre-industrial settlement pattern of the upper Ely Valley was one of scattered farms and hamlets, with the ancient town of Llantrisant - the church of the three saints - dominating the scene, both in terms of its physical presence on a hillside overlooking the valley, and also in its role as market centre for a wide rural area.

By the end of the 19th century railways had become synonymous with valleys in the South Wales coalfield, but early thoughts about the use of the Ely Valley for this purpose were hardly encouraging. On 21st September, 1829 James

Green, the eminent canal engineer, produced a report on the practicability of a tramroad linking the Marquess of Bute's property in the Rhondda Fawr Valley and around Llantrisant with Cardiff. A year earlier Green had prepared a plan of a new dock (later known as Bute West Dock) at Cardiff, which eventually opened on 9th October, 1839. Green had examined the course taken by the River Ely, but had not found it suitable as a route for horse-drawn tramroad:

> The most normal line for a railroad from these districts to the sea would be nearly the course of the River Ely which takes its rise only one mile and a half north of St John's Chapel (i.e. near present-day Tonyrefail) in the said valley and by a very circuitous course enters the sea near Pennarth, but I find the total rise of this river even if the ascent were graded over the whole line of railroad in this direction would be much more than is desirable for the most effectual road. To lessen this scale of ascent by intermediate inclined planes would be attended with great expense and the road would even then be very circuitous and would not intercept any minerals in its course and until its arrival in the immediate vicinity of Llantrissant.

Instead, Green recommended a route following that originally proposed in 1823 by George Overton, the engineer responsible for the construction of the Merthyr (or Penydarren) Tramroad. This was to pass via the Taff Valley and Llantwit Fardre to St John's Chapel, from where Green proposed an extension into the Rhondda Fawr Valley, via Penygraig. This scheme was to remain in contention for the next 10 or more years, but the only section to be built was that from the Taff Vale Railway, at Maesmawr, to Dihewyd Colliery, near Llantwit Fardre. This private line, known as the 'Llantwit Vardre Railway' and constructed by colliery owner Thomas Powell, was opened in April 1844.

The route offered by the lower part of the Ely Valley was to prove more attractive to I. K. Brunel, when planning the South Wales Railway (SWR). The SWR, as authorised by Act of 4th August, 1845, was to follow the valley of the Ely from Cardiff to what is now Pontyclun, before crossing over to the headwaters of the River Ewenni and taking that valley towards Bridgend. The original route then managed to avoid that important market town, but this oversight was quickly remedied by a further Act, passed in 1846. Built to Brunel's ill-fated broad gauge, the SWR was opened to passenger traffic between Chepstow and Swansea on 18th June, 1850. A station was provided for Llantrisant, but about two miles to the south-west of the town at the point at which the Llantrisant-Cowbridge turnpike road crossed the new railway.

The successful promotion of the SWR provided an incentive for a number of schemes for branch railways in the Parliamentary Session of 1846, at the height of the great 'Railway Mania'. These included the expansively titled 'Ogmore and Garw Vales and Port of Cardiff Union Railway' (O&GV&PCUR) and the 'Rhondda and Ely Valleys Junction Railway' (R&EVJR). The former was to run from the Ogmore and Garw Valleys, north of Bridgend, to Cardiff, via Pencoed and St Fagans, with a branch line serving the Ogwr Fach or Little Ogmore Valley, which lay between those of the Ogmore (Ogwr Fawr) and Ely. The R&EVJR was to leave the SWR at Llantrisant station, passing, via the Ely Valley and Penygraig, to the head of the Rhondda Fawr Valley, with a branch to join the Little Ogmore line of the proposed O&GV&PCUR. In many ways these early broad gauge schemes provided a preview of the railway network that was later to develop in the district to the north of the SWR.

The mineral wealth of the Rhondda Fawr was the clear objective of the R&EVJR, but at the time of its promotion there was little mining activity above Dinas for a railway to serve. The Rhondda branch of the TVR, opened on 10th June, 1841, terminated at Eirw-isaf (near modern Trehafod), where interchange was effected with the tramroad from Dinas. The question of extending the Rhondda branch beyond Eirw-isaf had been raised by a committee of TVR shareholders in August 1843, but it was not until 29th April, 1845 that their Directors ordered that steps be taken in this direction, and then for only by about a mile to a point near Porth, at the confluence of the Rhondda Fach and Rhondda Fawr rivers.

On 16th September, 1845 a notice was published announcing the promoters' intention of taking forward the R&EVJR, with the Prospectus being published later that month. This gave details of the Provisional Committee, consisting of 45 members, made up of South Wales industrialists, local landowners and individuals with interests in other 'Mania' railway companies, which had been formed to promote the railway.

The threat posed by this competitive broad gauge scheme appears to have concentrated minds somewhat. It was not, therefore, merely coincidental when, on the same day that this notice was published, the TVR Board resolved 'That a survey be immediately made of the various valleys which fall into the Taff', including those of the Rhondda Fawr and the Rhondda Fach. Plans for the various branch railways resulting from this survey were deposited in November 1845, and almost immediately the R&EVJR promoters sued for peace. On 22nd December, 1845 a letter was read at the TVR Board from Captain Dawson, Vice-Chairman of the Provisional Committee of the R&EVJR. Dawson suggested that if the TVR would guarantee to extend its line into the Rhondda Fawr, without delay, and advance £2,000 in consideration of the costs already incurred in the promotion of the R&EVJR, his committee would abandon any claim to the valley and hand over the plans and sections of its proposed railway to the TVR. However, the TVR Board, seeing no need to negotiate from its position of strength, rejected this proposition outright. With the subsequent abandonment of this competing proposal, the field was left clear for the TVR's Rhondda Fawr Valley extension, which was authorised by its Act of 26th August, 1846.

Like many schemes put forward during the Railway Mania there was little of substance to the proposed R&EVJR. However, within a few years developments in the Rhondda and Ely Valleys were to provide a much more encouraging environment for railway promotion. The 1850s saw the rapid growth of coal mining in the Rhondda Fawr Valley, spurred on by the completion of the TVR line through to what was to become Treherbert. On 21st December, 1855 coal from the Marquess of Bute's Cwmsaebron Colliery, at the head of the valley, passed over the Rhondda Fawr branch of the TVR. In January 1857 the TVR Board authorised the doubling of the Rhondda branch as far as Porth, and by February 1858 a total of eight collieries were reported to be sending coal out via the extension of the Rhondda Fawr line.

This period also witnessed the emergence of the Mwyndy haematite deposits as an important source of high grade iron ore. On 22nd October, 1852 the Bute mine, south of Llantrisant, re-opened, with May 1855 seeing the opening of the nearby Mwyndy iron ore mine. This ore was taken by road to Llantrisant station for transfer to the SWR.

Just over two miles to the west of Porth was a small side valley, known as Cwm Clydach. In November 1856 the TVR deposited plans for a short line of railway from the Rhondda Fawr line into this valley, with the Pwllyrhebog branch, as it became known, being authorised by the TVR Act of 17th August, 1857. It was not until 19th December, 1861, however, that the TVR accepted the tender of J.E. Billups for the construction of this line, which was opened for traffic in the early part of 1863. The Pwllyrhebog branch included a rope-worked inclined plane, with a gradient of 1 in 13, operated on the balanced load principle. This feature was necessary to overcome the substantial change in levels between the valley floor, occupied by the TVR, and the terminus of the branch higher up in Cwm Clydach. Although early mining activity in this locality was on a very small scale, Cwm Clydach was later to become a very important source of steam coal in its own right.

This general increase in activity also encouraged others to look to the adjoining Ely Valley as a potential source of mineral wealth. It was known that the valley contained the upper 'Llantwit' coal seams, together with the superior 'Rhondda' coking coal and black band ironstone. There were also hopes of discovering the much-prized steam coal measures in its upper reaches. The interest generated was summed up in a report in the *Cardiff & Merthyr Guardian* of 16th October, 1858, which stated that 'The Ely Valley is now seriously occupying the attention of capitalists as a desirable field of enterprise'.

Clearly, if there was to be any serious prospect of successfully exploiting the mineral wealth of the Ely Valley, then a railway would be needed. In addition, it appeared possible that such a railway could also make use of the gap in the hills at Penygraig to reach Cwm Clydach and the valley of the Rhondda Fawr, a tempting prize indeed!

Chapter Two

Promotion to Opening

On 4th October, 1856 the following notice appeared in the *Cardiff & Merthyr Guardian*:

ELY AND RHONDDA VALLEYS RAILWAY

A Company is being formed to construct a Railway upon the Broad Gauge principle, from the Llantrissant Station of the South Wales Railway, to join the Dare and Ammon Branch of the Vale of Neath Railway, with a Branch into the Rhondda Fawr Valley.

This notice, which was in the names of solicitors H. and W. Topgood of Westminster and R. W. Williams of Cardiff, went on to state that it was envisaged that, in the first instance, only some eight miles of the 'Main Line' of the Ely & Rhondda Valleys Railway (E&RVR), passing through the Ely Valley to Dinas (i.e. Penygraig), together with part of the Rhondda Fawr branch, terminating at Ystrad-y-fodwg Church, would be constructed.

Just over a month later, on 12th November, 1856, a Parliamentary notice, also signed by R.W. Williams, was published for the 'Ely Valley Railway'. This was to consist of a broad gauge line from Llantrisant station to Penrhiwfer (about 1½ miles north of Tonyrefail), a distance of just over 6½ miles, together with branches to Mynydd Gellyrhaidd and Glamychydd (also referred to as Castellau).

The background to this noticeable scaling down of the projected railway was revealed at a meeting of the EVR promoters, held in Cardiff on 15th November, 1856. In the absence of Earl Talbot, the Chairman of the proposed company, the meeting was presided over by his son, Viscount Ingestrie. Having outlined the relatively modest scope of the proposal, the Viscount observed that the EVR was 'essentially a landholders' line', and that the landowners had 'refused to listen to speculators who had attempted to interfere in its formation, and thereby to give a speculative character to it . . .'

According to Viscount Ingestrie, the railway, as now proposed, would assist in the development of the mineral resources of the Ely Valley at a very moderate cost in terms of construction and equipment, with half of the necessary capital having already been subscribed and other large subscriptions confidently expected. Expenses would also be contained by catering only for minerals and goods traffic, with a passenger service not being envisaged. The meeting concluded with the passing of a resolution to proceed with a Bill for the EVR in the following Session of Parliament.

Viscount Ingestrie's remarks at this meeting clearly indicate that the notice for the proposed E&RVR, published in October 1856, reflected the influence of 'speculators' rather than the needs of the landowners, as manifested in the proposal for the EVR.

A Prospectus for the EVR was published in December 1856. This gave details of the Provisional Directors, who, in addition to local landowners, also included

ELY AND RHONDDA VALLEYS RAILWAY.

A COMPANY is being formed to construct a Railway upon the Broad Guage principle, from the Llantrissent Station of the South Wales Railway, to join the Dare and Ammon Branch of the Vale of Neath Railway, with a Branch into the Rhondda Fawr Valley.

By means of this Railway a large and most valuable Mineral, Coal, and Iron District will be developed.

The undertaking will be divided into Sections, and in the first instance, eight miles of the Main Line, and three miles of the Branch only, will be constructed ; application for the necessarry powers will be made to Parliament in the ensuing Session.

These Sections will be the following :—

That portion of the proposed Main Line between its Junction with the South Wales Railway, through the Valley of the River Ely, to a point near Dinas, and that portion of the proposed Branch between its Junction with the Main Line, to a point near Ystrad-y-fodwg Church in the Rhondda Fawr Valley.

The great natural advantages which Cardiff possesses for shipping Minerals, are unquestionable. The demand for Coal is rapidly increasing, particularly for the South Wales Steam Coal. By this undertaking, Steam, House, and Coaking Coal, in which the Districts to be traversed abound, will be conveyed direct from the Pit's mouth to the various Depôts on the South Wales and Great Western Railways, at a less cost, and in a better and more saleable condition, than Coal which is subjected to a break of Guage in its transit.

The formation of the Ely Tidal Harbour at Cardiff, is also an important consideration in estimating the value of this Railway ; and it is believed that the present undertaking will be found to be highly remunerative.

The proposed Capital of the undertaking, together with further details, will be shortly announced. In the meantime communications on the subject may be addressed to Messrs. H. & W. TopGOOD, 16, Parliament-street, London, or to R. W. WILLIAMS, Esq., Cardiff.

September, 1856.

Notice in the *Cardiff & Merthyr Guardian*, 4th October, 1856, announcing the formation of the Ely and Rhondda Valleys Railway Co.

a number of influential South Wales industrialists. Prominent amongst the latter were Sir Ivor Bertie Guest, son of the late Sir Josiah John Guest of Dowlais Iron Works, Nash Vaughan Edwards of Rheola, near Neath, who had recently acquired the Mwyndy Iron Ore Mine, and ironmasters Rowland Fothergill of Abernant and George Thomas Clarke of Dowlais. One of the landowners, Evan Pritchard of Collena, near Tonyrefail, had also been listed as a member of the Provisional Committee of the proposed Rhondda & Ely Valleys Junction Railway in 1845. The Engineers were to be John Pyne of Canford, Dorset, who also acted as land agent to the Glamorgan estates of Sir Ivor Bertie Guest, and Edward David of Radyr, near Cardiff. The Solicitors were John Topham of Middleham, Yorkshire and R.W. Williams of Cardiff. Mr Williams was also to act as Secretary ('pro tem') to the company.

ELY VALLEY RAILWAY COMPANY

In conjunction and with the co-operation of the South Wales Railway Company.
Capital: £70,000 in 7,000 shares of £10 each. Deposit: £1 5s per share.

ENGINEERS
John Pyne Esq., Canford, Dorset.
Edward David Esq., Radyr, Cardiff.

SOLICITORS
John Topham Esq., Middleham, Yorkshire.
R.W.Williams Esq., Cardiff.

SECRETARY
(Pro Tem)
R.W.Williams Esq., Cardiff.

BANKERS
The National Provincial Bank of England, Cardiff.

PROSPECTUS

This Company is formed to construct a Railway upon the Broad Gauge principle from the Llantrissant Station of the South Wales Railway, to a point known as Penrhiwfer, with Branches from the Main Line, one extending into the CastellaValley and the other into the Gellyrhaidd Valley.

By means of this Railway a large and most valuable mineral, coal and iron district will be developed.

The great natural advantages which Cardiff possesses for shipping minerals are unquesionable and the demand for coal is rapidly increasing.

By this undertaking the coal, in which the Districts to be traversed abound, will be conveyed direct from the pit's mouth to the various depots on the South Wales and Great Western Railways at less cost, and in a better and more saleable condition than coal which is subjected to a break in gauge in its transit.

From the favourable reception accorded to the line by the South Wales Railway Company and the satisfactory arrangements made with the landowners, coupled with the low estimate for the construction of this line, when compared with other mineral lines now paying large dividends, it is evident that the proposed undertaking, having regard to the exceedingly valuable mineral fields which it will develop, must prove highly remunerative.

The larger portion of the Capital has already been subscribed.

Applications for the remaining shares may be addressed either to J. Topham Esq., Solicitor, Middleham, Yorkshire, or to Richard W. Williams Esq., Solicitor, Cardiff, in the form subjoined.

December 1856

The EVR Act received Royal Assent on 13th July, 1857, having encountered only limited opposition during its passage through the legislature. As well as incorporating the company and authorising the construction of the three railways shown on the Deposited Plans, the Act also provided for capital of £70,000, together with borrowing powers for a further £23,000. Two years were allowed for the compulsory purchase of land and three years for the completion of the works, both periods being unusually short for a line of this nature.

The first meeting of the Directors of the newly incorporated company was held on 22nd July, 1857. Earl Talbot was elected Chairman, with J.T. Hart as Deputy Chairman. One of the Directors, Richard Bassett of Bonvilston, midway between Cowbridge and Cardiff, was appointed Managing Director and Secretary, while Pyne and David were confirmed as the Engineers, and Topham and Williams as the Solicitors.

In addition to these appointments, two practical steps were also taken at this meeting. In the first of these, the Directors agreed to apply for further Parliamentary powers for a branch railway to serve the Mwyndy Iron Ore Mine, to the south of Llantrisant. This line could be continued to Brofiscin, about a mile to the east of the intended terminus, provided Earl Talbot contributed £1,000 towards the cost of the extension. Secondly, the Board decided to seek tenders for the construction of the authorised lines together with the newly proposed branch.

Plans for the Mwyndy branch were deposited in November 1857, the Act authorising the construction of this line receiving Royal Assent on 14th June, 1858, after passing unopposed through the legislature. This Act also provided for additional capital of £13,000 and further borrowing powers of £4,300.

The remainder of 1857 saw the completion of the various preliminaries prior to the start of work on the railway. On 14th August, 1857 the Engineers were instructed to prepare the necessary detailed surveys and working plans. This work took somewhat longer than expected, however, and it was not until the EVR Board meeting on 2nd October that John Pyne was able to report that the Engineers would be ready, on 16th of that month, to seek tenders for the works. At the same meeting instructions were given to prepare notices for a deviation of the line at Pant Glas, and for the acquisition of land for goods stations at the turnpike road crossing, near Lanely, at Tonyrefail and at or near the terminus of the Castellau branch.

Tenders for the construction of the railway were submitted to the EVR Board at its meeting on 6th November, 1857, when those of Messrs Giles, Logan and Waring Bros were referred for further consideration. The meeting was also informed that Earl Talbot had consented to the deviation of the line at Pant Glas. Having considered the short-list of contractors for the works at their meeting on 23rd December, the Directors agreed to negotiate further with Waring Bros. However, because of the unsettled financial climate it was not until the following January that this tender was formally accepted.

Start of work on the EVR was celebrated in the customary fashion with a ceremony of cutting the first sod. This event took place on Monday 17th May, 1858 in a field belonging to Lanely Fach Farm on Earl Talbot's estate, in front of what the *Cardiff & Merthyr Guardian* described as:

. . . a vast crowd of spectators, including persons of all classes, who naturally manifested the greatest interest in an event which promises to open up a new channel of access to one of the richest beds of minerals in the Principality.

The task of cutting and turning the first sod was performed by Mrs Clarke, wife of George T. Clarke of Dowlais Iron Works, one of the new company's Directors.

With work underway on the main line and the Gellyrhaidd and Castellau branches, there was also an urgent need to commence the Mwyndy branch in order to bring the valuable iron ore traffic onto the railway at the earliest opportunity. Little time was lost, therefore, after the passing of Mwyndy branch Act in June 1858, in seeking tenders for this work. On 19th July, 1858 the EVR Board accepted that of Waring Bros for the construction of the branch, but only as far as the Mwyndy iron ore mine.

At the company's half-yearly meeting on 23rd August, 1858 the Engineers were able to report that work had commenced in all cuttings for the first 2½ miles of the new line, and that the masonry of the first three river bridges and that over the turnpike road, near Lanelay, was in a forward state. At the next half-yearly meeting on 22nd February, 1859 further substantial progress was reported. All cuttings and embankments on the main line had been started and were being taken forward, with nearly one-third of the excavation having been completed. More than half of the masonry had been constructed, together with just over a quarter of the fencing. Over half of the required rails had been delivered, along with about a third of the sleepers. On a less positive note 'heavy and incessant rain' during the Autumn had retarded progress considerably.

The Mwyndy branch was in an even more advanced state, with the works completed except for about 3,000 cu. yds of earthwork near the junction with the main line of the EVR. In order to expedite the conveyance of iron ore it had been decided to lay temporary rails over this branch and rely on horses for haulage. On 16th November, 1858 two tenders received for such haulage were considered by the EVR Board and passed to Richard Bassett to arrange. The laying of the temporary rails as far as the Mwyndy iron ore mine was recorded in the report to the half-yearly meeting of shareholders on 22nd February, 1859, but traffic appears to have been worked for some time before this, as on that same day the EVR Directors were informed that the haulage contractor had given notice that he was unable to continue at the existing rate and had applied for an increase.

On 21st June, 1859 the works were inspected by a correspondent of the *Cardiff & Merthyr Guardian*, who commented favourably on the rapid progress being made with the new line. As well as recording that iron ore was being carried over the Mwyndy branch, he noted that 'the Castella Branch, with an elbow to Kimda (i.e. a short spur to Cwmdda, near the terminus of that branch), are showing themselves freely, and the line to Penrhiwfer is in a state of formation.' He also reported that work was in progress on the Gellyrhaidd branch.

The next half-yearly report, agreed by the Directors at their meeting on 25th July, 1859, gave details of further encouraging progress, with hopes being expressed that the line would be completed on time. However, the report concluded on a less optimistic note, possibly indicating some unease as to traffic prospects, by stating that:

> Since the date of the last report, coal has been reached at various points, and the approaching completion of the line makes it desirable that we should urge upon the coal proprietors the importance of increased activity on their part.

The Engineers clearly were pleased to record, in their report to the shareholders' half-yearly meeting on 7th February, 1860, that the works on the railway were nearing completion. Almost all of the earthworks had been completed, although great difficulty was still being experienced in getting through the hard rock cutting at Penrhiwfer. Ballast had been laid to within 30 chains of the terminus of the Gellyrhaidd branch, whilst the Castellau branch was ready for traffic. On the Mwyndy branch the temporary rails had been replaced with the permanent variety, although it would appear that the traffic was still being worked by horses. At Llantrisant the exchange sidings at the junction with the SWR, to the west of the station, had been laid, apart from the connection from these to the down main line.

The report concluded by noting that as soon as arrangements had been made with the colliery proprietors for the provision of sidings and staithes, the railway could be opened for traffic. On 11th June, 1860 the EVR Directors were informed that the remaining works, including the installation of a weighbridge at Llantrisant station and the erection of signals at various junctions, had been completed. Accordingly, Richard Bassett was instructed to take the steps necessary for opening the company's main line to traffic.

On 15th June the Joint Traffic Committee of the GWR and SWR agreed to provide an engine to work the Mwyndy branch iron ore traffic from 1st July. This was followed, on 13th July, by a similar agreement covering the EVR main line, which was to be effective from 1st August.

A formal ceremony to commemorate the opening of the main line was arranged for Thursday 2nd August, 1860, a special train being laid on to convey the Directors and officers of the EVR. This event created considerable interest in the district, the *Cardiff & Merthyr Guardian* recording that 'Flags were displayed in profusion; and the thriving little village of Ton-y-refail was the scene of much rejoicing'. The day also saw the first wagon loads of coal being sent down the line from Evan Pritchard's Collena Colliery, near Tonyrefail.

It will be recalled that only that part of the Mwyndy branch extending to the Mwyndy iron ore mine had been proceeded with in 1858. With the prospect of additional traffic from the remainder of this branch, John Pyne was instructed, on 8th March, 1860, to seek tenders for its completion. Once again Waring Bros were successful, their tender being accepted on 23rd August, 1860. The opening of the line to Brofiscin was recorded in the EVR's half-yearly report in February 1862 (MacDermot gives the opening date as 8th January, 1862). The report also noted that considerable additional expenditure had been incurred in constructing a viaduct to carry the railway over the workings of the Mwyndy Iron Ore Co.

While work was progressing on the construction of the EVR, a complex series of manoeuvres and negotiations was taking place in parallel, the results of which were to determine the future control of the company and its place in the railway network of South Wales. The choice of the broad gauge must have appeared an inevitable one to the EVR promoters in 1856, given that a junction was to be made with the SWR at Llantrisant station. However, as a broad gauge line the EVR would face considerable disadvantages, compared with the 'narrow' or standard gauge lines of the area. In particular, the relatively limited development of the broad gauge network meant that the ironworks in the northern parts of Glamorgan and Monmouthshire could only be reached by passing over standard gauge railways. As a result, coking coal and iron ore from the EVR, destined for these ironworks, was necessarily subjected to a break of gauge *en route*. There was also only limited accommodation for the broad gauge at the South Wales ports. Finally, there was a clear preference amongst colliery owners and other freight forwarders - the so-called 'Freighters' - for the smaller, more flexible standard gauge wagon.

When set against these disadvantages, a junction with the SWR was of relatively limited value. The broad gauge route to Merthyr was circuitous, passing via Neath and the Vale of Neath Railway, and still involved a break of gauge to reach the ironworks. The facilities for shipping from the broad gauge at Cardiff were very restricted. Direct access to London and the rest of the GWR's broad gauge empire, via the SWR, was initially of little benefit, although locomotive coal from Cil Ely Colliery, near Tonyrefail, destined for depots throughout that system, was later to become a very important source of traffic for the EVR.

These factors appear to have been appreciated clearly by another local company, which was, at the same time, anxious to develop new sources of traffic. The Ely Tidal Harbour and Railway (ETH&R) had been incorporated by Act of 21st July, 1856, to build a tidal harbour near the mouth of the River Ely, to the west of Cardiff, together with a connecting railway to the TVR at Radyr. A dock and change of name were authorised by Penarth Harbour Dock and Railway (PHD&R) Act of 27th July, 1857. The harbour was brought into use on 18th July, 1859, but, owing to delays resulting from the default of the contractors, Messrs Smith and Knight, the dock did not open until 10th June, 1865.

The attraction of traffic from the west appears to have been an early ambition of the ETH&R promoters, for on 6th December, 1855 they had decided to lay out their railway so that the 'Limits of Deviation', shown on its Deposited Plans, were contiguous with those of the SWR, where the two lines ran parallel between Canton and Ely, to the west of Cardiff. This would enable a junction to be made with the SWR at a future date without the need for further Parliamentary powers. The desire to attract traffic from the west was also evident when, at a meeting on 15th December, 1858, the PHD&R Directors decided to confer with their counterparts on the EVR Board regarding the possibility of a standard gauge connecting link between the railways of the two companies.

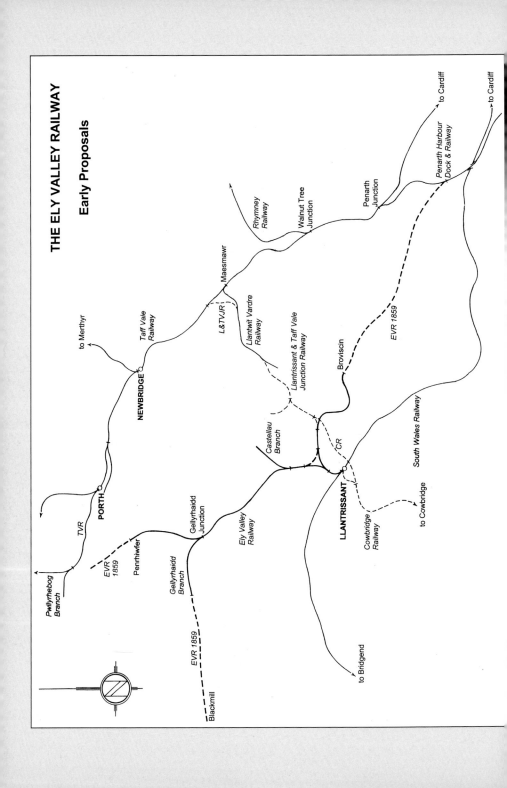

A PHD&R deputation, consisting of Directors John Batchelor and John Nixon, appeared before the EVR Board on 18th January, 1859. They presented two alternative proposals for a connection between the railways of the two companies: either by laying a third rail over the SWR between Llantrisant station and a junction with the Penarth Railway (as the PHD&R line was generally known), near Ely; or by means of an extension of the Mwyndy branch to a junction with the Penarth line, at or near Radyr. Having considered this proposition, the EVR Board decided to consult the SWR on the first option, it also being suggested that a joint EVR/PHD&R deputation should attend the SWR Board on 4th February. In the event, the full PHD&R Board declined to join in this deputation and decided instead to press for the second option for a connecting link. Having been informed of these developments at their meeting on 22nd February, the EVR Directors agreed that, as a matter of policy, their railway should be converted to the standard gauge and connected to the PHD&R by means of a mixed gauge section over the SWR. At the same time, the negotiations which were expected to follow were seen as a good opportunity to settle traffic arrangements with the SWR.

At first, the SWR responded positively to the EVR's overtures, which also dealt with the issues of rent and tolls for the use of its railway and Llantrisant station, together with the question of the capital required for the new works. The progress achieved through these negotiations was welcomed by the EVR Board when it met on 9th June, 1859. At the next meeting of the Board, on 25th July, a number of additional terms, put forward by the SWR, were also considered. These referred to the laying of the third rail right through to the Bute East Dock at Cardiff, with the EVR being granted running powers throughout, and the award of similar powers to the SWR over the EVR. These additional points were accepted by the EVR Directors, subject to a number of provisos, including an undertaking by the SWR to complete the standard gauge connection with the PHD&R on or before 2nd February, 1860. In addition, the SWR was to obtain the consent of the Great Western Railway to this arrangement, with a full agreement to be signed on or before 10th September, 1859.

The GWR's consent was needed because it had leased the SWR since December 1846, although the relationship between the two companies was not always harmonious. Unfortunately, the GWR was not impressed with the proposed arrangement, which it regarded as 'involving considerable expense without any adequate return as advantage'. As a result of this opposition, the SWR was obliged to withdraw from its negotiations with the EVR, this depressing news being reported to the latter company's Board at its meeting on 27th September, 1859. Anxious to retrieve something positive from this unhappy situation, the EVR Directors then instructed Richard Bassett to contact the SWR to establish if there was any prospect of it working the traffic of EVR or, alternatively, of the EVR working its traffic over the SWR. He was also to pursue the possibility of the SWR or the GWR either leasing or purchasing the EVR. No response was forthcoming on any of these points, however, and on 31st October the EVR Board reluctantly concluded that its negotiations with the SWR must be considered to be at an end.

With nowhere else to turn, the EVR Directors reverted to the idea of a direct railway between their line and the PHD&R, and agreed to prepare plans and notices for a Bill for such a scheme. These were deposited in November 1859 for the 1860 Session of Parliament. The Penarth Co., meanwhile, had not given up on its earlier ambitions, and accordingly was receptive to the EVR's approach. On 19th December, 1859 an EVR deputation attended the PHD&R Board to press it to contribute half the cost of the proposed connecting line, the total cost of which was put at £40,000. Having considered this proposition, at its meeting on 2nd January, 1860, the PHD&R Board agreed to subscribe £15,000 towards the cost of the proposed railway, subject to a satisfactory traffic agreement being entered into with the EVR.

Messrs Batchelor and Nixon returned to the EVR Board on 3rd January, 1860 to present the PHD&R's own terms for an arrangement between the two companies. They announced that the PHD&R was prepared to subscribe £15,000, subject to a share of any profits arising from the Penarth extension line. The Penarth Co. would also grant the EVR running powers over its railway, together with favourable treatment and accommodation at its harbour and dock. In return it sought running powers over the EVR, which in turn was to be converted to the standard gauge. In addition, the EVR was to undertake to build its Penarth line before commencing any other extensions. The EVR Directors did not respond on this occasion, but at the next meeting of the Board, on 7th February, 1860, it was agreed to negotiate with the PHD&R on the basis of that company's proposals.

The pressing need to secure an alternative arrangement, in the wake of the breakdown of negotiations with the SWR, appears to have clouded the judgement of the EVR Directors somewhat, and it soon became apparent that an over-optimistic assessment had been made of the resources likely to be available for constructing the Penarth extension. On 25th February, 1860 the EVR Board concluded that it would have to abandon this proposal unless a sum of £30,000 was subscribed towards the scheme. The Penarth Co. was clearly reluctant to see this happen and so agreed to increase its subscription to £20,000 and to withdraw its demand for a share of any profits from the extension line. In return, however, it sought two seats on the EVR Board.

Matters came to a head at the meeting of the EVR Board on 8th March, 1860. Richard Bassett reported that promises for a total of £27,000 had been obtained, of which £20,000 was from the PHD&R and £5,000 from the Mwyndy Iron Ore Co., with Crawshay Bailey, Chairman of the Penarth Co., undertaking to find the remaining £2,000 from other interested parties.

However, John Pyne, the EVR Engineer, advised that, in addition to this sum, the EVR would need to find at least £39,000 to complete the Penarth extension and convert throughout to the standard gauge. Faced with this information, the Directors agreed that, 'having regard to the financial position of this Company and to the still undeveloped state of the minerals of the district', the advantages of an arrangement with the PHD&R did not outweigh the cost of the extension line. As a result, it was decided to withdraw the Extensions Bill, with Richard Bassett being instructed to inform the Penarth Board that the decision had not resulted from any pressure from the SWR or 'any other interest'. However, this assurance does not sit easily with a comment, in the EVR half-yearly Report of

23rd August, 1860, that the Penarth extension had been abandoned because of the opposition it had aroused.

Despite this setback, there remained an urgent need to make some provision for working the traffic of the EVR, particularly as the railway itself was rapidly approaching completion. As a result, one other item agreed to at the meeting of the Board on 8th March, 1860 was that Richard Bassett endeavour to make temporary arrangements with the GWR or the SWR for this purpose. Bassett was well-placed to act as a 'go-between', as in March 1858 he had become a Director of the SWR. He was able to report the successful results of his negotiations to his fellow Directors on the EVR Board on 11th June. Under the proposed arrangement the SWR was to find the locomotive power (presumably from the GWR) and guards for EVR trains. The SWR would then work the traffic between Llantrisant station and the terminus of the Mwyndy branch, while the EVR would have the use of an engine for its main line traffic, at a rate to be agreed. The EVR was to be responsible for the maintenance of the permanent way. This proposal was accepted by the EVR Board and enabled the line to be opened for traffic on 2nd August, 1860.

At the next meeting of the EVR Board, on 27th June, 1860, Bassett was able to announce even more encouraging news: a proposal had been made by the SWR (effectively the GWR) to lease or purchase the EVR. The GWR's motives for this offer were made clear in a letter, dated 10th December, 1860, from its locomotive engineer, Daniel Gooch, to Richard Bassett, in which Gooch stated, in reference to the EVR, that 'Our object in taking the line would be chiefly for getting a connection to our own colliery and also to get, some day, into the steam coal not yet opened out'.

The colliery in question was that at Gyfeillon, near Pontypridd, the lease of which had been acquired by the GWR in 1854, from its owner John Calvert, for the supply of locomotive coal. In his earlier career as a contractor, Calvert had been responsible for a large portion of the original works on the TVR. According to Richard Bassett, the GWR's proposal had originated in a suggestion that the EVR should be extended to provide a broad gauge connection to Gyfeillon Colliery, independent of the TVR. Although there is little to indicate the route of such a line, it seems likely that it would have involved the extension of the Castellau branch, via Pontypridd.

It would appear that prior to this the EVR had also entertained ambitions in this direction, as evinced by a letter to the Editor of the *Cardiff & Merthyr Guardian* published on 19th May, 1860, which had bemoaned the fact that the EVR Directors had abandoned 'the branch railway proposed by them through the Castella and Gellywion Valleys to Pontypridd'. Unfortunately, the company's Minute Book is silent on this particular point.

The EVR Board responded to the SWR/GWR initiative by seeking the outright sale of its railway for £100,000. Negotiations soon got bogged down, however, as the GWR wished instead to take EVR shares and debentures to the value of £45,000, and to pay interest, rising to 4 per cent per annum over 5 years, on the remainder of the £100,000. The EVR countered by reducing the asking price to £90,000, but to no avail. Finally, in a desperate attempt to force a way out of this impasse, Richard Bassett was instructed, at the EVR Board meeting on 22nd October, 1860, to inform the GWR that if a definite reply was not received within a week, the negotiations would be considered to be at an end. Bassett was also to state that, in the event of their continuation, his Board would prepare and deposit plans for the Gyfeillon extension, subject to the expenses being borne by the GWR.

This ultimatum soon achieved results, although not necessarily those that the EVR Directors had in mind. On 1st November, 1860 the GWR Board authorised its Chairman, Lord Shelburne, to enter into an arrangement, if further negotiations proved satisfactory, for leasing the EVR. As the EVR was in no position to hold out for a better deal, agreement was soon reached, with the terms being accepted by its Board on 15th January, 1861, and by its GWR counterpart on 7th February of that year. Under this agreement, which was to be effective from 1st January, 1861, the GWR was to take a 999 year lease of the EVR, to acquire EVR shares to the value of £35,000 and to guarantee interest, rising to 5 per cent per annum over 5 years, on the balance of £80,000. Parliamentary authority for this lease was obtained in the Great Western, Hereford, Ross and Gloucester and Ely Valley Railways Act of 29th July, 1862.

The Gyfeillon extension was not taken any further, however, in spite of Richard Basset's assertion, in October 1860, that its promotion would counter the threat of the construction of a standard gauge railway from the TVR to Llantrisant. A proposal for such a line had been put to the TVR in September 1860, and its route was in the process of being surveyed when Bassett made his remark. The anxiety this prospect engendered in the broad gauge companies was evident on 3rd October when the EVR Solicitor, R. W. Williams, attended the TVR Board. Williams contended that any line from Llantrisant to the TVR should obtain the 'mutual sanction' of the TVR, EVR and SWR, and announced that the two broad gauge companies were willing to assist the TVR in such a project. The TVR's response was non-committal, its Chairman replying that whenever the companies concerned were ready to lay such a scheme before the TVR, his Board would be ready to receive it. However, once Williams had left the room it was agreed that the TVR shareholders would be advised to subscribe £10,000 towards a company, to be called the 'Llantrissant and Taff Vale Junction Railway', to build the line in question.

The plans for the L&TVJR were deposited in November 1861, with the subsequent Bill being opposed by the EVR. It was proposed that the L&TVJR would form a junction with the Mwyndy branch of the EVR at Maesaraul, south of Llantrisant. In addition, a separate branch line would run from the L&TVJR 'Main Line' to serve the Mwyndy iron ore mine. However, this line - the 'Mine Works Branch' - was soon struck out as a result of opposition from the EVR. In its place the L&TVJR was granted running powers from Maesaraul Junction to the 'south-eastern terminus' of the Mwyndy branch, over what was to become a section of mixed gauge railway. The precise meaning of the expression 'south-eastern terminus' was later to be become the subject of a long-running dispute between the L&TVJR and the GWR. The L&TVJR Act received Royal Assent on 7th June, 1861, bringing with it, for the EVR and its allies, the prospect of an unwelcome intrusion by a standard gauge railway into their broad gauge domain.

Chapter Three

Springboard for Expansion

The topography of the upper part of the Ely Valley provided a number of possible avenues for future expansion from the EVR. To the north the pass at Penygraig opened up the enticing prospect of an independent route from the Ely Valley into the heart of the Rhondda Fawr coalfield. Westwards, an extension from the Gellyrhaidd branch would open up access to the Ogmore Valleys and, further west, to those of the Garw and the Llynfi. For over 20 years these gaps in the hills were the scene of various attempts to reach the mineral wealth which lay beyond, with the EVR providing the springboard for expansion in both cases. However, the railway network that eventually emerged, although fairly comprehensive in its coverage, fell well short of the ambitions which had fuelled these years of Parliamentary struggle.

To the North

As has been seen, the idea of using the Ely Valley as a route into the Rhondda Fawr Valley had featured in a number of early schemes, but had been eschewed by the EVR promoters when seeking powers to build their railway. However, a northern extension, albeit in a much more modest form, was soon back on the agenda. On 27th September, 1859 John Pyne, the EVR Engineer, appeared before a meeting of his Directors with a plan and trial section of a continuation of the line from Penrhiwfer to Penygraig, a distance of just under a mile. In response, Pyne was instructed to make arrangements to take the scheme forward, provided not less than £4,000 was forthcoming from the landowners along the route. Plans for this extension were deposited in November 1859 in connection with the EVR's Bill for the 1860 Session of Parliament, but did not reach the statute book because of the company's decision on 8th March, 1860 to withdraw that Bill in its entirety.

Nevertheless, negotiations continued between the EVR and Waring Bros, the contractors, as to the best method for bringing about this extension. On 22nd October, 1860, the EVR Board agreed to enter into a private arrangement with the landowners along the route, whose consent had by then been obtained, together with Waring Bros, for the construction of the line. After some delay, while negotiations were concluded for the lease of the EVR, the Penygraig extension was built on such a basis, the cost being borne by the GWR, and the conveyances for the land involved being taken in the names of the Earl of Shrewsbury and Richard Bassett. MacDermot gives the opening date of this section as December 1862. However, a later GWR Minute refers to the line having been opened in 1863, while an agreement with a Mr Gethin concerning the road approach to the terminus at Penygraig (or 'Dinas' as it was called) is dated 23rd March, 1863.

The prospect of an incursion into its territory from the Ely Valley soon gave the TVR cause for concern. In a report to his Directors, dated 18th December, 1861, George Fisher, the TVR's General Superintendent, expressed fears that, following the leasing of the EVR by the GWR, a scheme could be expected to be promoted for the extension of that line into the Rhondda Fawr Valley, and, 'in all probability', on to Aberdare. However, it was not until November 1865 that proposals of this sort emerged, although when they did they appeared to give credence to Fisher's worst fears.

Under its 'Further Powers' Bill, deposited for the 1866 Parliamentary Session, the GWR sought authority for a railway from Penrhiwfer to the head of Cwm Clydach at Clydach Vale. This was intended to provide a statutory basis for the railway line already existing between Penrhiwfer and Dinas, but for the TVR the continuation beyond Dinas represented an intrusion by a competitor into its precious domain in the Rhondda Fawr Valley, albeit into part of a side valley which the TVR itself had yet to penetrate.

Also proposed for the same Session was an altogether more ambitious scheme, the 'Ely Valley and Vale of Neath Junction Railway' (EV&VNJR). Promoted by colliery owners David Davies and Ebenezer Lewis, the EV&VNJR was to run from a junction with the EVR, near Penrhiwfer, to Blaenrhondda, at the head of the Rhondda Fawr Valley, but not, it should be noted, on into the Vale of Neath. At this date David Davies was in the process of sinking the Parc and Maendy Collieries, near Treorchy, with the steam coal being struck at the latter place on 9th March, 1866. Ebenezer Lewis was similarly engaged at Tynewydd Colliery, near Treherbert. In his report to his Directors of 14th December, 1865, George Fisher was succinctly dismissive in his summing up of the EV&VNJR, noting that 'generally the scheme appears to be got up for the benefit of two coal proprietors'. Nevertheless, the EV&VNJR could have proved a potent threat to the TVR's interests, especially if it had been associated with the proposed Barry harbour and railway schemes also authorised in the Parliamentary Session of 1866.

Both the Dinas-Clydach Vale line and the EV&VNJR were subsequently withdrawn under an arrangement entered into between the GWR and the TVR, whereby a 'depot' was to be provided in Cardiff for coal from the TVR destined for London. This suggests a possible GWR involvement in the promotion of the EV&VNJR, as does a TVR Minute, dated 18th May, 1866, which refers to the GWR 'undertaking to withdraw their contemplated Ely Valley Extension and Ely Valley and Vale of Neath Branches'. This arrangement left only the already constructed line from Penrhiwfer to Dinas to be authorised by the GWR (Further Powers) Act of 30th July, 1866.

In 1866 there was only very limited mining activity in Cwm Clydach for an extension from the EVR to serve. The Pwllyrhebog branch of the TVR terminated just beyond the top of the rope-worked incline, with private siding connections to two small collieries, D. & E. Thomas's 'Cwm Clydach' and Bush & Co.'s 'Blaen Clydach'. However, a much larger development was anticipated in 1871, with the formation of Thomas, Riches & Co. to sink a colliery further up Cwm Clydach at Clydach Vale. On 6th January, 1871 the new company applied to the TVR for an extension of the Pwllyrhebog branch to the site of the proposed colliery. This application was approved in March of that year, and, on 10th November an agreement was entered into between the TVR and Thomas, Riches & Co. for the construction of the line. Under this agreement the colliery company was to build the Pwllyrhebog branch extension, and then transfer the freehold of the land involved to the TVR. Significantly, Thomas, Riches & Co. also undertook to send all the produce of their projected colliery out via the TVR.

Sinking of Clydach Vale Colliery commenced in 1872, with the connecting railway being completed during the following year. To raise it up to the height of the colliery, the new line was constructed with a 'zig-zag', just beyond the top of Pwllyrhebog incline. The TVR's ownership of the Pwllyrhebog branch extension was confirmed by its Act of 13th July, 1899.

The Pwllyrhebog incline, worked at this time solely on the 'balanced load' principle, was hardly an efficient method of serving what was to become a large-scale colliery. In spite of this handicap, the TVR Board persistently refused to sanction the installation of a stationary engine to increase the incline's capacity. An extension from the EVR, on the other hand, would not encounter quite such an unfavourable change in levels in order to reach Clydach Vale Colliery. It was not long, therefore, before such a proposal emerged, with plans being deposited for the 'Ely and Clydach Valleys Railway' (E&CVR) in November 1872. This line was to run from a junction with the EVR, just below its terminus at Dinas goods station, to the head of Cwm Clydach, a distance of about 2 miles. The influence of another company was not hard to discern, however, with Richard Bassett being prominent amongst the promoters of the proposed railway.

The GWR's involvement in the proposed E&CVR was made clear on 13th December, 1872, when its Board agreed to support the promotion of the line. In spite of TVR opposition the E&CVR Act was passed and received Royal Assent on 5th August, 1873.

Another scheme with GWR backing, also promoted in the 1873 Parliamentary Session, proved rather less successful. The 'Pontypridd and Ely Valley Junction Railway' (P&EVJR) was put forward by a combination of local interests and speculators to connect the EVR, south of Tonyrefail, with the hub of the TVR system at Pontypridd, together with a north to west curve at Gellyrhaidd Junction. However, in this case the GWR agreed to support only that part of the scheme extending from the junction with the EVR to a point near Treferig House, to the east of Tonyrefail. On 6th March, 1873 the promoters announced their intention of abandoning the remainder of the Bill, leaving the resulting Act to be confined to a branch line of just over a mile long, together with powers to enter into working and traffic agreements with the GWR. In spite of the GWR's support and encouragement nothing more was heard of this truncated proposal.

For George Fisher the promotion of the E&CVR provided clear evidence of the GWR's avaricious intentions towards the Rhondda Fawr. His suspicions were further aroused by news of the presence of GWR surveyors on the ground to the north of Penygraig. Reporting this development to his Directors on 30th October, 1874, Fisher advised that, as a counter-measure, plans and notices should be prepared for a branch railway from the company's Rhondda Fawr branch to a junction with the EVR. In the event, Fisher's fears proved ill-founded, at least as far as the 1875 Session was concerned, but in the longer term the uneasy truce was destined not to last.

By the mid-1870s the growth of the coal export trade had led to severe congestion and delays at Cardiff Docks. Pressure mounted for improved facilities, but on 2nd November, 1876 such requests were brushed aside when the third Marquess of Bute wrote to Cardiff Chamber of Commerce refusing to make Roath Dock, which had been authorised by Act of 16th July, 1874. This rebuff led directly to a proposal for a new dock at Barry, together with a connecting railway to the South Wales main line at Peterston. Plans for the dock and railway (which was to follow the route authorised by the abortive Barry Railway (Alteration) Act of 1866) were deposited in November 1876.

The burst of activity which followed the receipt of the Marquess's letter appears to have led to a marked increase in the unease already being felt by officers and Directors of the TVR. On 9th November, 1876, its Board gave instructions for notices and plans to be prepared, if found necessary, for a short line of railway between the company's Rhondda Fawr branch and the Ely Valley line, near Penygraig. Less than a week later, on 14th November, a Parliamentary notice was issued for the 'Ely and Rhondda Valleys Junction Railway' (E&RVJR), which was to run from the E&CVR, north of Penygraig, to Blaenrhondda. Then on 17th November, in what seemed, at first sight, to be a counter-move on the part of the TVR, a notice appeared for the 'short line' from the Rhondda Fawr branch to the EVR. However, according to a Minute of its Board meeting on 30th November, 1876, the GWR, having received notice of the TVR's intention to proceed with this proposal, had responded to the threat by producing plans for the E&RVJR. This notification must have occurred prior to the publication of the TVR's Parliamentary notice, which suggests that the TVR had been panicked into a pre-emptive move, which had in turn triggered the GWR's response. The GWR's involvement in the promotion of the E&RVJR was confirmed on 14th December, 1876, when its Board agreed the names of the Directors to be included in the Bill. Prominent on this list were J.S. Gibbon, then Chairman of the EVR, and Richard Bassett.

Regardless of which company made the first move, George Fisher was convinced that the E&RVJR and the Barry scheme were but two parts of a single assault on the TVR's domain in the Rhondda Fawr. In his report of 7th December, 1876 he commented that 'A glance at the map will suffice to show that the E&RVJR must be part of the entire (i.e. Barry) scheme and in my opinion they must stand or fall together'. However, at this stage Fisher does not appear to have been aware of the exact nature of the GWR's role in the promotion of the E&RVJR.

Meanwhile the Barry promoters, led by J.D. Treherne of Cardiff and R.F.L. Jenner of Wenvoe, were attempting to interest the GWR in their dock and railway scheme. On 14th December, 1876 the GWR Directors indicated that, whilst they were favourably disposed towards the construction of the railway proposed between Peterston and Barry, they were unwilling to support the proposed dock. Attitudes had hardened by 18th January, 1877, when the GWR refused to take responsibility for the proposed railway unless the construction of the dock had first been secured. This effectively was the end of this attempt to promote a dock and railway at Barry. The Bill itself was not deposited and it was to be another seven years before a successful scheme was inaugurated following the incorporation of the 'Barry Dock and Railways' in August 1884.

The Bill for the E&RVJR was lodged, but was withdrawn before its second reading, following a meeting between officers of the GWR and the TVR on 13th February, 1877, which restored the uneasy peace between the two companies.

The final attempt to use the Ely Valley line as a springboard into the Rhondda had its origin in events in the western part of the County of Glamorgan. In the 1881 Session an abortive attempt was made to promote the 'Rhondda and Swansea Bay Railway' (R&SBR), from Treherbert to Swansea. A modified scheme in the following Session proved more successful, with the company being incorporated by Act of 10th August, 1882. The R&SBR Bill had been opposed by the GWR, which had also countered with a scheme of its own designed to provide a western outlet for the coal of the Rhondda Fawr.

Under the GWR (No. 2) Bill, plans for which were deposited in November 1881, three lines were proposed: Porth-Tonyrefail; Tonyrefail-Hendreforgan; and Kenfig Hill (on the Tondu-Porthcawl line) to the South Wales main line, to the west of Pyle. The first of these railways would have involved a tunnel, 3,199 yds long, under Mynydd y Glyn between Tonyrefail and Porth, with a gradient up from the junction with the TVR of 1 in 80 against the load. Despite strong objections from the TVR, this unlikely scheme was authorised by Parliament, the Act receiving the Royal Assent on 24th July, 1882. Nothing practical resulted from this enactment, however, with all but the Tonyrefail-Porth line being abandoned in 1891 and that section following in 1894. On seeing the notice for the final abandonment Bill, Ammon Beasley, the TVR General Manager, summed up his company's relief by stating, 'It is altogether to our interest that this line should be abandoned; and we can have nothing to say in opposition to the Bill.'

Thus of all the many attempts to enter the Rhondda Fawr Valley from the south, via the EVR, the only line to be built was the E&CVR, authorised in 1873, and this barely touched the valley proper. The fundamental problem faced by all such proposals was that the entrance from the Ely Valley was at a much higher level than the valley floor of the Rhondda Fawr. As a result, any railway attempting this route would have been at a serious competitive disadvantage, compared with the TVR, because of the need to raise coal up from the collieries, which were mostly on the valley floor, to the higher level of the intruding line. The alternative, espoused by the GWR's scheme of 1882, was to give the railway a heavy gradient against the load, once again imposing a considerable handicap on any such proposal.

To the West

The potential of the side valley to the west of the Ely, just below Tonyrefail, had been recognised early on with the inclusion of the Gellyraidd branch in the plans for the EVR, deposited in November 1856. It was not long after the EVR's Act of incorporation in July 1857 that a westward extension of this line first came under active consideration. On 12th August, 1857 a meeting took place in London between Richard Bassett and Directors of the Llynvi Valley Iron (LVI) Co. to establish what support that company might give to a proposal to extend the Gellyrhaidd branch to its iron works at Maesteg. These works were served by the Llynvi Valley Railway (LVR), as successor to the Duffryn Llynvi and Porth Cawl Railway, a 4 ft 6¾ in. gauge 'edgeway' originally incorporated in 1825. Under its Act of 15th June, 1855, the LVR had been re-incorporated with powers to build a replacement broad gauge line from Bridgend to Tywith, north of Maesteg. However, it was not until May 1858 that the company invited tenders for the construction of the new line. The LVI Co., meanwhile, had become increasingly restive at the LVR's lack of progress, so much so that in June 1857 it applied for legal powers to compel the company to put its railway in good order, in this case by building its authorised new line.

This dispute provides the context for the negotiations which took place between the EVR and the LVI Co. By September 1857 little had been achieved, and on 2nd October of that year a letter from the Chairman of the LVI Co. was read to the EVR Board, declining to proceed with the suggested extension. When work commenced on the LVR new line in June 1858, much of the incentive for the promotion of a railway from Gellyrhaidd to Maesteg was lost. The new broad gauge railway was opened for goods and mineral traffic on 10th August, 1861, and for passengers between Bridgend and Maesteg only on 25th February, 1864.

Discussions also took place in the autumn of 1857 with James Brogden concerning the possibility of a more modest extension of the Gellyrhaidd branch, as far as his Tondu Iron Works. However, once again the necessary support was not forthcoming, and on 6th November, 1857 the EVR Board decided not to proceed with this proposal.

Another scheme to extend the Gellyrhaidd branch emerged towards the end of 1859. On 31st October, 1859 this question was discussed by the EVR Directors, leading to an instruction to the company's Solicitors and Engineers to prepare notices and plans for a Bill in the ensuing Session of Parliament. Plans were deposited in the following November for a new line from the terminus of the Gellyrhaidd branch, at Hendreforgan, to Blackmill, together with a branch line to Gilfach Goch in the Little Ogmore Valley. This Bill also sought powers for the Penarth and Penygraig extensions already encountered in this narrative. Needless to say, the Gellyrhaidd extension proposal, like the other extensions in the Bill, was soon found to be equally over-ambitious. The proposed line between Hendreforgan and Blackmill was the first to go, being abandoned in January 1860. Then, on 25th February, 1860, the EVR Board agreed that the Little Ogmore branch would also be withdrawn, unless £10,000 was subscribed towards the cost of its construction. Finally, on 8th March of that year, this line too was abandoned, as a result of the EVR Board's decision to withdraw the entire Extensions Bill.

Following the leasing of the EVR by the GWR in 1861, the next proposal for an extension from the Gellyrhaidd branch took the form of an independent promotion, the 'Ely Valley Extension Railway' (EVER), plans for which were deposited in November 1862. This scheme involved the construction of a line from Hendreforgan to a junction with the LVR at Tondu, with branches up the Little Ogmore Valley to Gilfach Goch, and from Blackmill to the head of the Ogmore Valley. Promoted by Richard Bassett, together with fellow EVR Director Nash Vaughan and H. Llewellyn, the EVER was surveyed by Henry Voss, then recently appointed by the GWR as Manager and Engineer of the EVR. The EVER, therefore, appeared to have strong connections with both the EVR and the GWR. However, when the EVER proposal was considered at the EVR Board on 17th December, 1862, the Directors of that company refused to make any subscription towards the proposed undertaking, although they did agree that every other assistance should be given, and that the company should petition Parliament in support of the EVER Bill. As for the GWR, no suggestion of its involvement with this scheme has been found prior to June 1864, when its Chairman was authorised to arrange terms for working the EVER.

Also deposited in November 1862 were plans for the 'Ogmore Valley Railways' (OVR) from Tondu, via Blackmill, to what is now Nantymoel at the head of the Ogmore Valley. The OVR was promoted by the firm of John Brogden & Sons to serve extensive mineral property which that company had leased in the Ogmore Valley. The ensuing Parliamentary struggle saw the OVR being favoured at the expense of the EVER lines west of Hendreforgan, which were then withdrawn, leaving the OVR intact to be authorised by Act of 13th July, 1863. The Act providing for the construction of the rump of the EVER, from the terminus of the Gellyrhaidd branch at Hendreforgan to Gilfach Goch, received Royal Assent on 28th July, 1863. This left a railless gap between Hendreforgan and Blackmill, which was to become the subject of protracted contention in later years. The EVER was granted powers to enter into working and traffic agreements with the EVR and the GWR and for the laying of mixed gauge track over its authorised railway.

From the start, the OVR promoters appear to have appreciated the limitations of the broad gauge in South Wales, and were, therefore, determined to adopt the standard gauge. Unfortunately, for a branch line connected, via the LVR, to the broad gauge South Wales main line at Bridgend, this decision brought with it isolation for the OVR from the rest of the standard gauge network of South Wales. To overcome this disadvantage either the GWR would have to convert its intervening railways to mixed gauge or an independent standard gauge line would need to be built between the OVR and the standard gauge system. The OVR's first move indicated a preference for the former course, but with the latter as an acceptable alternative, which could be employed with advantage in any subsequent negotiations with the GWR. As early as October 1863, Henry Voss had informed Daniel Gooch, Locomotive Superintendent of the GWR, that the Brogdens wished to know if his company would lay a third rail over its lines between Bridgend and Cardiff. If not then the Brogdens threatened to seek an alternative arrangement with the TVR. In spite of this possibility, the Brogdens' request was rejected when it was considered by the GWR Board on 29th October, 1863.

Even though this issue remained unresolved, the OVR Board decided, on 4th May, 1864, to proceed with the construction of its authorised railway (reported to be ready for traffic on 11th August, 1865). However, at the same time preparations were also made to promote the construction of a rail link between the OVR and the EVR. In August 1864 James Brogden again wrote to Henry Voss on the subject of laying a third rail over the EVR and the South Wales main line between Llantrisant station and Cardiff. Voss's reply of 30th August was diplomatically non-committal, noting that the GWR Board 'are by no means indisposed to extend the narrow gauge over portions of their broad gauge system where the special circumstances of the case seem to justify it and the prospect of a fair return on the outlay can be shown'.

A subsequent offer from the Brogdens of financial assistance towards the cost of this proposal also failed to elicit a sufficiently positive response from the GWR. In the circumstances, therefore, the OVR had little choice but to deposit plans for standard gauge railways from Blackmill to the PHD&R and the TVR for consideration in the 1865 Session of Parliament.

The TVR, meanwhile, had also been casting its covetous eyes towards the Ogmore Valleys. In November 1864 the company came forward with a proposal for a connection between its main line, at Willowford, between Taffs Well and Treforest, and the EVR, making use of the recently completed L&TVJR, both in a physical sense and as a proxy in the subsequent Parliamentary battle.

A Bill was also deposited for a line from Hendreforgan to Blackmill, to be known as the 'Ely and Ogmore Valleys Junction Railway' (E&OVJR). The fact that the E&OVJR was promoted by Richard Bassett and Henry Voss suggests a possible GWR/EVR involvement in this scheme, but the minute books of the two companies do not provide further enlightenment on this point.

Intriguingly, Voss, together with former EVR Engineer John Pyne, was also actively engaged at this time in the promotion of another railway scheme, involving a line from a junction with the South Wales main line at Peterston to Barry, where the two engineers had also proposed the construction of a dock. Again, it is unclear whether Voss was representing, in some way, the GWR interest, or simply acting in a freelance capacity. With a dock at Barry, an alternative outlet for Ogmore coal might have been possible by making use of the E&OVJR and this first Barry Railway, as the latter's Act, which received the Royal Assent on 5th July, 1865, also included powers for the laying of a third rail over the South Wales main line, from Llantrisant station to the junction at Peterston (and on to Newport). Henry Voss's involvement in the Barry scheme did not last long, however, as, later that month, he resigned as Engineer, his place being taken by Henry Bolden. It was Bolden who prepared plans for a new harbour at Barry, together with a realignment of the Peterston-Barry line (the 'Alteration' Act) and a branch line from Cadoxton to join the Penarth Railway at Cogan (the 'Extension' Act), all of which were authorised in the 1866 Session of Parliament.

But to return to the 1865 Session: none of the proposals relating to the Ely and Ogmore Valleys achieved the Parliamentary success of the Barry scheme of that year. The OVR and L&TVJR Bills were rejected during their passage through the legislature, whilst that for the E&OVJR was withdrawn. Despite its success in the House, however, this first Barry Railway was unable to attract the necessary support in the outside world and was subsequently abandoned by Board of Trade warrant, dated 5th August, 1874.

The 1866 Session saw the various companies returning to the fray for a repeat, in many ways, of the previous year's contest. The OVR and the TVR, once again through the medium of the L&TVJR, put forward modified schemes designed to connect the Ogmore Valley to the docks at Cardiff and Penarth and to the inland markets for coking coal. The GWR also entered the field in its own right with a west to east curve at Mwyndy Junction, together with three short links between its South Wales main line and the PHD&R, to the west of Cardiff station.

Plans were also deposited, under the name of the EVR, for railways to connect its Gellyrhaidd branch, at Hendreforgan, with the OVR at Blackmill, together with a link from its main line, at Ynysymaerdy, to the Common branch of the L&TVJR, north of Llantrisant. All was not as it seemed, however, for when this Bill was brought before the EVR Directors on 21st February, 1866, considerable surprise, not to say outrage, was expressed that it had been deposited 'without their knowledge and sanction'. They also found it to be, in all respects, 'highly objectionable and detrimental to their property and interests'. The Bill, in fact, had been deposited by the GWR using the EVR's name, but without its consent. On 27th February, 1866, in a somewhat belated attempt at diplomacy, Frederick Saunders, Secretary of the GWR, wrote to Richard Bassett, stressing that it had not been his company's intention to harm EVR interests, and offering to add such clauses to the Bill as would be necessary for the protection of those interests. Despite these assurances, however, the Bill itself was fatally wounded and was subsequently withdrawn by the GWR.

The confrontation of 1866 proved to be more productive than that of the previous year, at least as far as the authorisation of new railways was concerned. The spoils were divided along broadly territorial lines, with the L&TVJR and GWR proposals being approved in full, whereas only that section of the OVR between Blackmill and Hendreforgan was sanctioned. Royal Assent was given to the L&TVJR and OVR Acts on 23rd July, 1866, with the GWR (Further Powers) Act following on the 30th of that month.

Legislative success was not matched by progress on the ground, however, with the result that in 1870 the Llynvi and Ogmore Railway (L&OR) (which had been created by the amalgamation of the OVR and the LVR, authorised by Act of 28th June, 1866) revived the plan for a link from its system to the standard gauge network. The 1871 Session, therefore, witnessed a dramatic attempt by this company to break out of broad gauge encirclement by means of a direct standard gauge line from Blackmill to join the Rhymney Railway, north of Walnut Tree Junction. The TVR responded by depositing plans for the 'Ely and Ogmore Valleys Junction Railways' (not to be confused with the similarly named scheme of 1865), intended to bridge the long-disputed Blackmill-Hendreforgan divide. Fortunately, sanity prevailed and both schemes were quickly withdrawn in consequence of the GWR's decision to convert its broad gauge railways in South Wales to the standard gauge and its offer to enter into traffic agreements with the other companies concerned.

Looking ahead, the Hendreforgan-Blackmill line was opened on 1st September, 1875, while of the L&TVR New Lines, the extension of the Common branch through to a junction with the EVR opened on 25th February, 1875, with the Common Branch Junction-Penarth Railway link ('Llantrisant No. 1 Railway') eventually opening on 11th September, 1886.

Thus, this protracted Parliamentary struggle did at least bring forth a fairly comprehensive railway network, when compared with the results of the similar amount of promotional effort aimed at the Rhondda Fawr Valley, over roughly the same period.

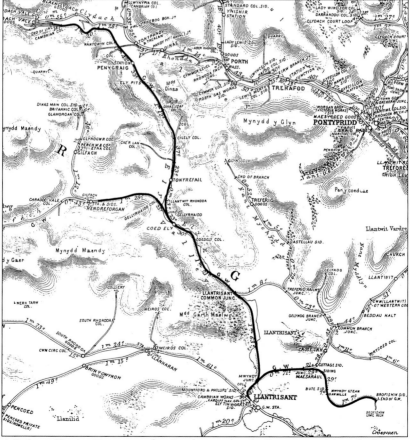

A Railway Clearing House map showing the completed railway network in and adjoining the Ely Valley - some way short of Parliamentary ambitions.

Chapter Four

Goods and Minerals Only

By its lease of the EVR in 1861 the GWR acquired a somewhat impoverished single line system, albeit, as has been seen, one with undoubted strategic potential. Traffic, on the other hand, was somewhat slower to develop. George Fisher of the TVR, commenting on the GWR's Leasing Bill, deposited for the 1862 Session of Parliament, felt that the GWR 'must have some object in view beyond simply leasing a line upon which the traffic receipts do not represent 25 per cent of the cost of the working expenses'.

To look after its new acquisition the GWR appointed one of its engineers, Henry Voss, as Engineer and Manager of the EVR, thereby relieving Richard Bassett of the job of Managing Director of the railway. However, Bassett continued to be very active as a Director of the EVR, the South Wales Railway (until 1863), and the GWR (from 1863), and also as a promoter, with or without GWR support, of various railway schemes in the area. Initially Voss was based at the Engineer's Office at Llantrisant station, but he was later transferred to Gloucester, with responsibility for the South Wales main line between Grange Court Junction, near Gloucester, and Llantrisant, in addition to the EVR.

Consideration was also given to the best way of operating the EVR. On 1st October, 1862 the GWR Board agreed that it should be 'worked in connection with and in continuation of the South Wales Railway', under the superintendence of Frederick Saunders, Secretary of that company.

For a brief period the EVR was in the unusual position of being leased by a company the nearest outpost of which was over 60 miles away. This soon changed, however, when the SWR, which had been leased by the GWR since December 1846, was absorbed by the larger company under powers contained in the GWR (South Wales Amalgamation) Act of 21st July, 1863, these being effective from 1st August of that year.

It will be recalled that the Llantrissant & Taff Vale Junction Railway Act of 1861 had provided for the laying of a third rail over the Mwyndy branch of the EVR, between Maesaraul Junction and the 'south eastern terminus' of that branch. Shortly after the passing of this Act in June 1861, however, a dispute arose between the companies concerning the interpretation of the 'south eastern terminus'. The GWR, as lessee of the EVR, took this to be the terminus of the branch as at the time of the passing of the L&TVJR Act, i.e. Mwyndy Iron Ore Mine, whereas the L&TVJR contended that it meant the 'Parliamentary' terminus, i.e. Brofiscin. As a result, the GWR refused to lay the third rail until this point had been clarified.

This issue was not resolved until 8th April, 1863, when the GWR obtained the opinion of leading railway Counsel J.H. Lloyd on the matter. When Mr Lloyd took the view that the 'south eastern terminus' must be that shown on the deposited plans for the Mwyndy branch, (i.e. Brofiscin), the GWR conceded and entered into negotiations with the L&TVJR for laying the third rail on and granting running powers over the mixed gauge section between Maesaraul

Junction and Brofiscin. The resulting agreement was dated 9th January, 1864, but there was still a considerable delay before the third rail was laid over the branch, with the standard gauge connection through to Brofiscin not opening until 5th December of that year.

Accommodation for standard gauge traffic between Maesaraul Junction and Llantrisant station was the subject of a separate agreement, also dated 9th January, 1864, between the GWR and the Cowbridge Railway (CR) Co. The CR had been incorporated by Act of 29th July, 1862, to build a standard gauge line from the L&TVJR, just above Maesaraul Junction, to Cowbridge, with a short spur to the SWR west of Llantrisant station for the interchange of goods traffic. The authorised railway was to bridge the SWR just east of Llantrisant station, and was to have its own passenger station at right angles to that of the SWR. However, following a meeting in Paddington on 5th November, 1862 between representatives of the Cowbridge Co. and Richard Bassett and Frederick Saunders, it was agreed that this direct line should be abandoned in favour of the adoption of mixed gauge on the EVR between Maesaraul Junction and Llantrisant station, with running powers over this section being granted to the CR. These arrangements were confirmed by the agreement of 9th January, 1864, already referred to.

The CR was to be worked by the TVR, with the passenger train service running between Pontypridd, Llantrisant and Cowbridge. Formal opening for goods traffic took place on 30th January, 1865, with regular goods trains from Cowbridge working over the standard gauge connection to Maesaraul Junction from 8th February of that year. Inspection of the entire route between Llantrisant Junction (south of Treforest) and Cowbridge for passenger use was undertaken by Captain Rich for the Board of Trade on 22nd and 23rd March, 1865. Rich's report on that part of the EVR between Maesaraul Junction and LLantrisant station revealed that instead of simply laying the third rail on this broad gauge section, a somewhat more complicated arrangement had been adopted:

> The new narrow gauge line commences at Llantrissant Station on the SWR, where it crosses the main line of that railway on the level and runs up to the south side of the down line platform.
>
> From Llantrissant Station to the Mwyndy Branch Junction of the EVR a distinct narrow gauge line is laid alongside the broad gauge line. At the Mwyndy Junction the narrow gauge line joins the broad gauge line of the Mwyndy Branch and forms a mixed gauge line, up to the junction with the L&TVJR at Maesaraul.
>
> The new narrow gauge passenger line is single throughout and is about 1 mile 45 chains long. The mixed gauge portion being about 1 mile long and the single narrow gauge about half a mile. Land has been purchased and the bridges have been constructed for a double line of rails. The bridge rail is used at the junction with the L&TVJR and at the Junction with the SWR and a single-headed rail in chairs on the intermediate portion. The rails are fastened with fang bolts. The sleepers are longitudinal under the bridge rail, and transverse under the other rail which is fished and fixed in a joint chair.
>
> The only works on this line are one underbridge with a wooden top and masonry abutments and a viaduct of four openings, two of which are spanned with wrought iron girders and two with cast iron girders, resting on masonry piers and abutments. These works appeared substantial and of sufficient strength. . . .

Captain Rich found that the junction between the EVR and the L&TVJR at Maesaraul was incomplete and badly sited and required the provision of a proper raised signal cabin. The arrangements at Llantrisant station were also considered to be unsatisfactory. As a result, he recommended that Board of Trade sanction should not be granted for the use of the EVR line by passenger trains, a conclusion he also reached in the case of the L&TVJR. Because of a protracted dispute concerning the responsibility for carrying out the necessary alterations, it was not until 29th August, 1865 that Rich was able to recommend, following re-inspection, that Board of Trade approval should be given for the use of the line between Llantrisant station and Maesaraul Junction for passenger traffic. TVR passenger trains started running over this section, *en route* to and from Cowbridge, on 18th September, 1865, although, at first, the daily service between Pontypridd and Llantrisant amounted to a meagre two trains, each way.

Another problem affecting the Mwyndy branch also came into prominence at about this time. The viaduct, which had been built to cross part of the Mwyndy Iron Ore Co.'s workings, was found to be unstable, as a result of undermining by that company. On 12th November, 1863, the GWR Board, having been informed of this state of affairs, concluded that the safety of this viaduct remained the responsibility of the EVR, but also agreed to give the local company every assistance in dealing with the problem. In a report, completed on 21st October 1864, Henry Voss and Samuel Dobson, a consulting engineer who was also engaged in that capacity by the PHD&R, put forward three possible solutions: to relocate the viaduct; to replace it with an embankment; or to divert the railway onto the iron ore company's land. Although Voss and Dobson favoured the third option, it would appear that the second, involving replacing the viaduct with an embankment, was the one that was carried out.

The passing of the Ely Valley Extension Railway Act in July 1863 brought with it the prospect of additional coal traffic from the valley of the Little Ogmore, via the Gellyrhaidd branch of the EVR. Despite being promoted by, amongst others, Richard Bassett and engineered by Henry Voss, it was not until 22nd June, 1864 that any formal GWR interest in the EVER manifested itself. This took the form of a resolution authorising the company's Chairman, Richard Potter, to arrange terms for working the line. Unfortunately for the GWR this intervention came too late. The firm of John Brogden & Sons had purchased shares in the new undertaking, and when the contractor, Mr Lumley, failed, the Brogdens were able to step in and complete the works on the railway. This action led directly to the absorption of the EVER by the OVR, this being confirmed by the Ogmore and Ely Railways (Amalgamation) Act of 5th July, 1865. However, in the absence of a rail link between Hendreforgan and Blackmill, the EVER was to remain, for about 10 years, isolated from the rest of its new parent system. Accordingly, an arrangement was made for the GWR to work the traffic of the EVER, via the Gellyrhaidd branch of the EVR. Thus although the EVER had been built as a mixed gauge line, it was destined to be used only by broad gauge trains until the gauge conversion in 1872. The new railway made an end-on junction with the Gellyrhaidd branch, immediately to the east of the site of the later Hendreforgan station.

The EVER was opened for minerals traffic only on 16th October, 1865, bringing much-needed additional traffic onto the EVR. On 16th March, 1872 one of these coal trains was derailed in spectacular fashion at Hendreforgan, the accident resulting in the death of the guard. In his report to the Board of Trade, F. H. Rich, by now a Lieutenant Colonel, found that the derailment had been caused by poor track, combined with excessive speed by a heavy train.

The 1860s were not a good time for the GWR or for railways leased by the company. Its financial position had been deteriorating for some time, but these troubles were compounded by the Overend, Gurney & Co. bank crash of 10th May, 1866 and the panic which followed. Under the Chairmanship of Daniel (later Sir Daniel) Gooch, who had been elected to this position on 2nd November, 1865, the GWR embarked on a policy of rigid economy, with capital projects scaled down, deferred, or abandoned, and running costs pared to an absolute minimum.

This extreme stringency soon made its mark on the EVR, and, in particular, its permanent way. On 9th November, 1866 Henry Voss reported that the longitudinal sleepers and transoms laid down in 1860 were 'much decayed', and that one branch laid with Barlow rails was in a 'thoroughly used up state'. As it was intended to convert the EVR to standard gauge, Voss recommended that the line should be relaid with transverse sleepers. This suggestion was accepted by the GWR Board at its meeting on 6th December, 1866, but unfortunately for Voss and the EVR, the Directors also decided to refrain from ordering any sleepers! Voss was obliged, therefore, to make do as best he could. Later that month he advocated taking up the rails on the Castellau branch for use elsewhere on the EVR. There was then little, if any, traffic on this line, it having been reported in the *Cardiff Times* of 12th February, 1864 that 'The Castella Colliery of Dr Lloyd is nearly exhausted'. Voss's recommendation was accepted by the GWR Directors on 31st January, 1867, but it was requested that the landowners be informed of the reasons for this decision and of the company's intention of relaying the branch as soon as circumstances permitted.

In the event, the Castellau branch was never relaid, although looking ahead for a moment, its reopening could have taken place had the GWR been prepared to support the promotion of the Treferig Valley Railway in 1878. On 24th October, 1878 the GWR Board rejected such an approach from the promoters of this scheme, but, nevertheless, indicated that it would be prepared to relay the Castellau branch in connection with the proposed railway. Following this rebuff, the Treferig Valley Railway was taken forward with TVR support, the line being authorised by Act of 21st July, 1879 and opened in April 1883. A short spur was laid from the Treferig Co.'s 'main line' to an end-on 'junction' with the defunct Castellau branch, but this was never used for traffic. The Castellau branch itself was not formally abandoned until the passing of the GWR Act of 4th August, 1926.

The financial crisis of 1866 also delayed the conversion of the GWR's broad gauge lines in South Wales to the standard gauge. Powers for this change had been sought in the company's 'Further Powers' Bill, deposited for the 1866

Session, with specific reference being made to the EVR. In his report to GWR shareholders of 2nd March, 1866 Daniel Gooch noted that 'There is no doubt it has become necessary for us to look the matter of the narrow gauge fairly in the face'. During the previous week the company had received a 'Memorial' from 'nearly every firm of any standing in South Wales' seeking such a change.

The Further Powers Act received Royal Assent on 30th July, 1866, by which time the consequences of the Overend, Gurney Bank crash, earlier in the year, were only too apparent. Gauge conversion was put in abeyance where it remained until August 1870, when the GWR re-affirmed its intention of converting the EVR and the section of the South Wales main line between Llantrisant station and Newport to the standard gauge. However, this relatively modest proposal was soon overtaken by a much grander design. In the company's report of 25th February, 1871 it was announced that it was intended instead to convert all broad gauge lines between Swindon and Milford Haven to standard gauge, with the mixed gauge being provided between Swindon and Didcot.

Gauge conversion on the South Wales main line and its branches was arranged for May 1872. According to working instructions issued on Saturday, 11th May, broad gauge traffic on the main line was to cease that night, with the first standard gauge trains operating on the following Monday. A locomotive coal train had worked up from the EVR to Swindon on the preceding Friday. However, complete conversion was not effected until 29th May.

The work on the EVR itself involved narrowing the broad gauge section between Llantrisant station and Dinas, together with the Gellyrhaidd branch to the end-on junction with the mixed gauge EVER, from which the third (i.e. broad gauge) rail was removed. However, the changes on the Mwyndy branch were rather more complicated. As has been seen, there was already an independent standard gauge line between Llantrisant station and Mwyndy Junction, provided for the benefit of TVR trains. During gauge conversion the points at Mwyndy Junction were removed, thereby creating two parallel single lines - the Ely Valley main line and the Mwyndy branch - between Llantrisant yard and the divergence of these two lines at the site of Mwyndy Junction. The third rail was then removed from the mixed gauge section from that point to the terminus of the Mwyndy branch at Brofiscin.

The arrangement of the running lines between Llantrisant yard and the site of Mwyndy Junction, described above, did not last long, however. On 23rd June, 1874 Colonel Rich completed his report of inspection for the Board of Trade on the new layout between these places. A double junction had been installed at Mwyndy Junction, enabling normal double line working to be introduced between there and Llantrisant yard. Colonel Rich was satisfied with the arrangements and recommended that they be approved.

After giving up the lease of Gyfeillon Colliery, near Pontypridd, in 1865, the GWR obtained its locomotive coal under contract from various other collieries for a number of years. On 8th April, 1874 Sir Daniel Gooch presented the GWR Board with details of Cil Ely Colliery, north of Tonyrefail, the lease of which had been offered to the company by colliery owner, David Davies. This offer was accepted and Cil Ely went on to become a major supplier of locomotive coal for the GWR. According to his diary, Sir Daniel visited the mine on 12th September, 1876, travelling up via the Rhondda Fawr branch of the TVR and returning by way of the EVR. On 19th July, 1877 the GWR Board ordered that the first of many excursions be run, free of charge, for the benefit of workmen employed at Cil Ely Colliery, the destination on this occasion being Chepstow.

By 1874 the EVR was serving, in addition to Cil Ely, a number of other important collieries, including Collena, Dinas Isaf, Penrhifer and Penygraig, all situated on the section of the main line above Tonyrefail. Gilfach Goch and Dinas Main Collieries on the EVER also produced substantial tonnages for the railway.

Production of haematite iron ore from the Mwyndy field peaked in the early 1870s, but then declined in the face of competition from ore imported from Spanish sources. The Bute mine passed from Messrs Levick, Simpson & Fothergill to the Dowlais Iron Co. in June 1873, before ceasing production in 1881. The Mwyndy Iron Ore Co's mine closed in 1884, having produced over a million tons of ore during the previous 20 years. Llwyn-sear, a much smaller affair, had closed in 1865, but was re-opened by the Mwyndy Iron Ore Co. between 1884 and 1891. Iron ore traffic also passed over part of the Mwyndy branch, *en route* to the TVR, from Llanharry (1863-74) and Trecastle (1878-1891) on the Cowbridge branch. This category of traffic was not to return until the first ore was dispatched from the modern mine at Llanharry in 1910.

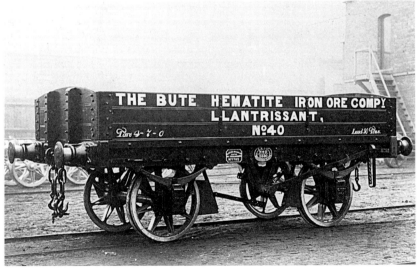

An early iron ore wagon belonging to the Bute Hematite Iron Ore Co.
Author's Collection

Although the Ogmore Valley Railways Act of 1866 had authorised the construction of a railway between Blackmill and the EVER at Hendreforgan, the successor company, the Llynvi & Ogmore Railway, showed no great urgency in starting work. The scheme was kept alive by the passing of an extension of time Act on 24th June, 1869, but it was not until January 1871 that the L&OR accepted the tender of Mr Hanson for its construction. In March 1872 the GWR, anticipating the early completion of this line, gave notice that it would cease to work the traffic of the EVER, via the Gellyrhaidd branch, from May 1873. However, work on the new railway was repeatedly delayed through a combination of bad weather, shortage of labour and poor ground conditions over part of the route, with the result that it was not until 15th October, 1874 that notice of intention to open the line for passengers was forwarded to the Board of Trade. Coal traffic appears to have operated before this date, but the opening to passengers did not take place until 1st September, 1875, as a result of the failure of the GWR to provide necessary materials and to carry out certain works required prior to the introduction of such a service. This delay was then compounded by the refusal of the Board of Trade to sanction the line for passengers, following the first inspection in April 1875, until certain alterations had been carried out.

The Blackmill-Hendreforgan line had been projected as part of a route for coal from the Ogmore Valley to Penarth and Cardiff Docks, but was destined to see very little through traffic. Instead, its main roles were as an alternative outlet for coal from the Little Ogmore Valley and as a route for the passenger service between Blackmill and Hendreforgan, which was extended to Gilfach in 1881.

A northern extension from the Ely Valley line, from Dinas to Clydach Vale, was foreshadowed by the passing of the Ely & Clydach Valleys Railway Act in 1873. Just over a year later, on 20th August, 1874, the GWR Solicitor was instructed to take the steps necessary for giving effect to this Act. The token nature of the E&CVR's independence was apparent when, later that year, the Directors named in its Act, with the exception of Richard Bassett, were replaced by GWR nominees. However, it was not until 15th April, 1875 that the GWR Board ordered the construction of the line to be proceeded with, and tenders to be sought for the work. On 17th June, 1875 the E&CVR Board received the detailed plans and specifications for their new railway, prepared by consulting engineers Dobson, Brown and Adams. The Directors also accepted the tender of J. Briggs for the construction of the first stage, from Dinas to Clydach Vale Colliery. This was followed, on 31st August, 1875, by approval of the draft of an agreement with the GWR for the working of the line. Preparation of plans and specifications for the second stage of the works was ordered at the meeting of the E&CVR Board on 6th January, 1876. Once again Mr Briggs was successful in bidding for the contract, with his tender being accepted on 15th March of that year.

The E&CVR was to leave the Ely Valley line just before Dinas goods station. A replacement station was needed on the new line as the existing facility was to be given up to the Penygraig Colliery Co. On 21st June, 1876 the E&CVR Chairman reported that it would be necessary to have three lines of rails and a

Cambrian Colliery, Clydach Vale, c. 1910.   *Author's Collection (courtesy R.H. Marrows)*

A view of Cambrian Colliery *c.* 1910, illustrating its elevated position in Cwm Clydach, high above the Rhondda Fawr Valley. The line of 'Cambrian' wagons is loaded with pit props for use in the mine.   *Ian Pope Collection*

roadway at the site of the proposed goods station, and on 13th December the GWR authorised the station's construction, complete with goods shed, office and cattle pen.

The new railway was approaching completion when on 6th January, 1877 the GWR's Divisional Superintendent, T. I. Allen, went over part of it and commented that it was 'not in good order and needs a good deal of ballasting'. On 30th August, 1877 the E&CVR Board accepted a recommendation from Dobson, Brown and Adams that maintenance of the line should be placed in the hands of the GWR Engineer, suggesting that by this time the works had been substantially completed.

According to MacDermot, the E&CVR was opened for goods traffic on 10th August, 1878, but this may refer only to the new goods station at Dinas and the section of line leading to it. It was to be some time before the rest of the new railway saw any traffic. Although the primary objective of the E&CVR was the Clydach Vale Colliery of Thomas, Riches & Co., the agreement between that company and the TVR, dated 10th September, 1871, had stipulated that all coal produced by the colliery should go out via the Pwllyrhebog branch. In the event, it was not until 9th February, 1882 that the GWR Board sanctioned expenditure on a connection between the E&CVR and the Clydach Vale Colliery sidings. Two days earlier the *Western Mail* had reported that on 6th February, 1882 'a locomotive ran for the first time along the EVR . . . to the top of the Clydach Valley'. The earliest private siding agreement between the GWR and Thomas, Riches & Co., which has come to light, is dated 1st December, 1885.

A coal wagon built for Thomas, Riches & Co in 1888, with dumb buffers at one end and the sprung variety at the other.   *Author's Collection*

Cambrian Colliery, Clydach Vale *c*. 1910.   *Author's Collection (courtesy R.H. Marrows)*

The E&CVR was vested in the GWR by Act of 6th August, 1880, with the financial arrangements being approved by the E&CVR Board on 27th of that month.

Clydach Vale Colliery was to become a major source of coal traffic for the Ely Valley line, with a third shaft being sunk in 1889. The three pits were producing over 3,000 tons per day by the end of the century, by which time they were known as Cambrian Nos.1, 2 and 3. A number of other collieries were opened in the Ely Valley in the last quarter of the 19th century, including Nantgwyn and Ely at Penygraig, whilst existing collieries at Cil Ely, Collena and Dinas Isaf were greatly enlarged. The resulting growth in coal traffic, coupled with that produced by the collieries of the Little Ogmore Valley, led to increasing congestion on the single track railway and to pressure for its doubling.

A break with the early days of the EVR occurred on 17th January, 1891, with the death, at the age of 70, of Richard Bassett at his home at Highclere, near Newbury. A Deputy Lieutenant for the County of Glamorgan and a JP, he had remained a Director of the EVR and of the GWR, but had been in declining health for some time.

Chapter Five

Passengers at Last

The promoters of the EVR had made it quite clear, at the outset, that they had no wish to cater for passenger traffic on their proposed railway. Without the complications which such a service inevitably would bring, they could get on with the main business of life - moving the coal from the pits. In spite of the substantial increase in the population of Tonyrefail and the upper reaches of the Ely Valley which followed the growth of the mining industry, it was to be nearly 40 years, from the opening of the line through to Dinas for goods traffic, before regular passenger trains would run between Llantrisant and Penygraig.

On 1st September, 1875, in what was to prove something of a token gesture towards the travelling needs of the nearby mining communities, the GWR opened a passenger station at Hendreforgan, in what can, without fear of contradiction, be described as 'the middle of nowhere'. This station was about about a mile from Gilfach Goch and nearly two miles from Tonyrefail, situated in a lonely and desolate spot, devoid of almost all human habitation. Its location, coupled with the need for passengers to change trains at Blackmill and the fact that the people of Gilfach Goch and Tonyrefail tended to look to Rhondda Fawr rather than to Bridgend, meant that Hendreforgan station was destined to do little to improve the lot of local travellers. The extension of the Blackmill-Hendreforgan service to Gilfach on 9th May, 1881 brought the trains nearer to one of the local centres of population, but this was of little use to the inhabitants of the Ely Valley.

Shortly after the opening of Hendreforgan station the GWR's Divisional Superintendent, T.I. Allen, wrote to his General Manager, James Grierson, on the subject of passenger trains on the EVR. In his letter, dated 22nd September, 1875, Allen pointed out that such a service would require the doubling of the section between Mwyndy Junction and Gellyrhaidd Junction. The upper part of the line, on the other hand, could remain single, thereby avoiding the expense of altering the many colliery sidings. Allen's conclusions highlighted the fundamental problem which, for the next 25 years, was to stand in the way of the introduction of a passenger train service on the Ely Valley line. The single line, above Mwyndy Junction, would suffice for goods and minerals traffic alone for many years, despite of the constant growth in coal output. However, the running of passenger trains would necessitate the doubling of at least part of this section, thereby making their introduction a very expensive matter. It was not until the growth of coal traffic reached a point where doubling could no longer be avoided, that accommodation for passengers could be contemplated.

Towards the end of 1876 the GWR received the first of many formal requests for the introduction of a passenger train service over the EVR. Commenting on this 'Memorial' from residents of the area in a letter to James Grierson, dated 14th December, T. I. Allen confirmed that the 'want . . . is very greatly felt', especially in the populous upper parts of the valley, where the inhabitants were wholly dependent upon the delights of Hendreforgan station or the nearest Rhondda Fawr branch stations of the TVR. He was also confident that the running of passenger trains would 'ultimately be very remunerative to the Company'. Nevertheless, despite this optimistic assessment, the GWR Directors felt unable to countenance the expenditure involved in such a change, and, therefore, rejected the 'Memorialists'' request at their meeting on 3rd January, 1877.

Another petition, signed by the 'principal gentlemen and tradesmen of the neighbourhood', was considered by the GWR in November 1883. By this date Allen had become convinced that it was desirable to double the line between Mwyndy Junction and Gellyrhaidd Junction, and to rearrange the sidings at Llantrisant, whether or not a passenger service was introduced. He estimated that such a service would bring in a revenue of nearly £4,700 per annum, with the cost of the necessary improvements being put at just under £20,000. This time the question was considered important enough to justify an inspection of the line by James Grierson and Henry Lambert, the GWR's Chief Goods Manager, but once again the Directors were reluctant to commit the expenditure required. A further Memorial, this time from the inhabitants of Penygraig, Dinas, Williamstown, Tonyrefail and adjoining districts, was submitted in November 1888, but met with a similar response.

With the growth of the mining industry in the upper reaches of the Ely Valley, and the consequent increase in the area's population, the 1890s saw mounting pressure for the opening of the railway to passengers. Towards the end of 1891 the GWR received a request from Mr A.J. Williams, MP for the South Glamorgan constituency, for such a service. By this date the mineral traffic had reached a scale where passenger trains could only be accommodated by doubling of the entire line between Mwyndy Junction and Penygraig station (as Dinas had been renamed in April 1885). Coupled with improvements needed at Llantrisant station, this raised the cost of the opening to passengers to about £60,000. Not unexpectedly, the GWR Board concluded, at its meeting on 12th November, 1891, that this substantial outlay could not be justified.

From its establishment in 1888, Glamorgan County Council had pursued a vigorous policy aimed at securing the provision of passenger train services on the various goods-only lines lying within its administrative area. The Ely Valley line was an obvious contender for the Council's attention, and, on 17th October, 1892, its Clerk, Mr T. Mansel Franklin, wrote to the GWR requesting that steps be taken to cater for passenger traffic on the line. In response, the company's Traffic Committee, at its meeting on 26th November, 1892, ordered that plans be prepared showing the works that would be necessary in order to accommodate passenger trains on the EVR.

The County Council soon grew impatient, however, and on 8th August, 1893, Mansel Franklin wrote again to the company, this time threatening to take the matter to the Railway Commissioners. This letter was considered by the GWR Board on 10th August, 1893, when it was agreed to inform the Council that a passenger service was not possible because the EVR was a separate concern, only leased by the GWR, that the proposal would entail heavy expenditure and that neither company possessed the necessary powers. However, the Council was also to be advised that the question would be kept under review and that enquiries would be made regarding the terms for land acquisition and the possibility of contributions from the colliery owners towards the cost of altering colliery junctions.

Henry Lambert, the GWR's General Manager since the death of James Grierson in 1887, conveyed this decision to the County Council on 14th August, 1893. However, the company was sufficiently concerned about the threat of referral to the Railway Commissioners for it to seek the opinion of leading railway Counsel, C.A.Cripps QC, on the subject. Cripps took the view that it was likely that the Commissioners would make an order compelling the GWR to introduce a passenger service on the EVR, as had happened in the recent case of Willesden Local Board vs. the Midland Railway Co.

On 28th November, 1893 the County Council carried out its threat and took its complaint to the Court of the Railway and Canal Commission. The Council contended that the GWR was monopolising the Ely Valley line for goods and minerals traffic to the exclusion of passengers, and, accordingly, applied for an order to compel the company to afford 'all reasonable and proper facilities' for passenger traffic. In its view passenger stations were needed at Clydach Vale, Penygraig, Penrhiwfer, Tonyrefail and Gellyrhaidd Junction.

Plans were prepared by the GWR showing the alterations that it considered would be necessary to meet the County Council's demands. These included a new double track section from the Cambrian Colliery siding to the end of the Ely and Clydach Valleys line, at Clydach Vale, where a two-platform terminal station, complete with locomotive turntable, was envisaged. An interchange station at Gellyrhaidd Junction was also seen as necessary.

The case came before Mr Justice Collins, the Rt. Hon. Sir Frederick Peel and the Rt Hon. Viscount Cobham, sitting in the Queen's Bench at the Royal Courts of Justice, Westminster, on 12th April, 1894. C.A.Cripps QC, on behalf of the GWR, was now able to argue that it would be impossible to order the conveyance of passengers without first ordering the construction of stations and the doubling of the line, and that this, as the Appeal Court had ruled, in the case of Hastings Town Council vs. South Eastern Railway Co., was outside the jurisdiction of the tribunal.

The County Council responded by asserting that the case should be heard on its merits and that there was clearly a need for passenger trains on the Ely Valley line. James Hurman, formerly Traffic Manager of the TVR, appearing in support of the Council, felt that the railway was already well-adapted for this purpose and that the gradients, although severe, were no worse than those found on other valley lines in South Wales.

T.I. Allen, giving evidence for the GWR, was of the opinion that doubling of the line was essential for the safe conduct of a passenger service. This view was given considerable weight by Major Marindin, a Board of Trade Inspector who was to be Chief Inspecting Officer from 1895 until his death in April 1900. Major Marindin told the court that he felt that the greater part of the works specified by the GWR would need to be in place before such a service could be sanctioned.

The GWR's case also received support from what, on other occasions, would have been a somewhat unexpected source, Ammon Beasley, General Manager of the TVR. Beasley was, of course, not without interest in the matter as a passenger station at Penygraig would be directly competitive with those at Dinas and Llwynypia on the TVR. He argued that the upper part of the Ely Valley was already well-served by the two stations named, and that, in any case, only 10 per cent of the passengers at those stations were booked through to Cardiff. In addition, the TVR provided a frequent through service to Cardiff, whereas a similar journey, via the EVR, would require a change of trains at Llantrisant, with fewer trains to chose from.

Having listened to the arguments, Mr Justice Collins gave judgement on behalf of the Commission on 19th April, 1894. He found that the facts of the case fell within the limits set by the Court of Appeal in the Hastings case, referred to earlier. The running of passengers trains on the Ely Valley line would require the doubling of the line, but the Railway Commissioners did not have the power to order this work to be done. The County Council's application, therefore, was dismissed with costs.

This outcome was a cause for congratulations all round when it was reported to the GWR Board on 3rd May, 1894. It had confirmed an important principle and was felt to be of 'great value' to the company. However, just over a month later the Directors may well have had their attention drawn to comments on this case made by the President of the Board of Trade, Mr J. Bryce, in the House of Commons on 8th June. In response to a question from A.J. Williams MP, Mr Bryce noted that Lord Cobham had remarked, after the judgement, that 'I hope that the time will shortly arrive when the converting of this line into a passenger line may commend itself to the Company as a matter of profit and of interest to themselves.' Whilst the Board of Trade did not have the power to intervene, Mr Bryce was in no doubt that the GWR would wish to give 'due consideration to an opinion emanating from such a quarter'.

Just over a year later, on 31st July, 1895, the GWR General Manager, Henry Lambert, addressed his Traffic Committee on the subject of the Ely Valley line. Lambert reported that a considerable increase in traffic had taken place and that for some time the existing arrangements had been found to be 'quite inadequate'. Accordingly, he recommended that the railway be doubled between Llantrisant Common Junction and Gellyrhaidd Junction, with passing loops provided on the remaining single track sections, at Penrhiwfer and at Penygraig, together with an improved gradient at the summit of the line at Penrhiwfer. This was agreed to by the Committee, and on 11th December, 1895 the tender of John Mackay was accepted for the work. The additional line between Llantrisant Common Junction and Gellyrhaidd Junction was brought into use on 20th September, 1896.

The next section to be taken in hand was that between Gellyrhaidd Junction and Penygraig. On 28th October, 1896 the new General Manager, Joseph Wilkinson (Lambert having retired through ill-health in the preceding July), presented plans of this proposal to his Traffic Committee. He also advised taking the additional line 23 feet deeper at the Penrhiwfer summit, which, whilst increasing the construction cost by nearly £20,000, would produce a saving, in working expenses, of nearly £6,700 a year. These improvements would also permit the running of passenger trains on the Ely Valley line.

Earlier that year a report had been prepared by the company's officers advocating the introduction of such a service. This report referred to the history of repeated applications for stations to serve Clydach Vale, Penygraig, Tonyrefail and Gellyrhaidd Junction, and for trains to connect Gellyrhaidd Junction with Hendreforgan and Gilfach, but recommended that stations be opened only at Penygraig and Tonyrefail, leaving the Penygraig-Clydach Vale and Gellyrhaidd Junction-Hendreforgan sections to be dealt with 'at some future date'. It was estimated that 45,280 tickets would be sold annually at Penygraig, together with a further 63,626 at Tonyrefail.

In November 1896 the GWR published a Parliamentary Notice for a Bill, which was to include powers for widening the line between Penygraig and Gellyrhaidd Junction, together with the alteration of levels on certain sections. In addition, powers were to be sought to make the Ely Valley line 'fit and proper' for passenger traffic. These powers were obtained under the GWR (Additional Powers) Act of 6th August, 1897.

On 10th February, 1897 the GWR Traffic Committee accepted a recommendation that the doubling of the line between Llantrisant Common Junction and Mwyndy Junction be carried out. Within days of the passing of the Additional Powers Act in August 1897, the Committee also agreed to proceed with the works required for the introduction of a passenger service, including the provision of stations at Penygraig and Tonyrefail and major alterations at Llantrisant, together with the doubling the remaining sections of single line. This action was confirmed by the full Board on 7th October, 1897, with the cost of the works being estimated as £63,495.

Board of Trade approval for the plans prepared for these alterations was sought and provisionally obtained in December 1897, but it was not until 25th March, 1901 that the company was able to submit notice of its intention to open the line to passengers. The Board of Trade granted provisional sanction for the use of the line by passengers following the receipt of a further notice, dated 16th April, 1901, announcing that the works were complete and ready for inspection.

Provisional sanction enabled passenger trains to be introduced, on 1st May, 1901, in advance of the Board of Trade inspection of the line. The inaugural train, the 7.40 am from Penygraig, carried a large complement of passengers who thronged aboard at that station and at Tonyrefail, with many more well-wishers along the line.

The inspection of the passenger railway was conducted by Colonel H.A. Yorke, his report of 21st May, 1901 stating:

This line, which has hitherto been worked as a mineral line only, has recently, under the powers obtained by the Company in their Act of 1897, been doubled and converted into a passenger railway, and an inspection of it therefore became necessary.

The line commences at its junction with the main line near Mwyndy Signal Box at 182 miles 9.15 chains from London, and terminates, as far as passenger traffic is concerned, at the north end of Penygraig Station, its length being 6 miles 62.2 chains.

Beyond Penygraig Station the line is continued as a mineral line and was not inspected.

The line is double throughout, and no land has been acquired for any further widening. The gauge is 4 feet 8½ inches.

The steepest gradient has an inclination of 1 in 50.30, and the sharpest curve a radius of 20 chains.

The permanent way is laid with bull-head steel rails weighing 92 lbs per yard, cast iron chairs weighing 46½ lbs each and creosoted sleepers 9 feet by 10 inches by 5 inches, which are placed at a maximum distance of 2 feet 11 inches from centre to centre. The ballast is of broken stone and slag and the 'road' is in excellent condition and fully suitable for passenger traffic.

There are 13 bridges under the line, and 4 over the line. Of the under-bridges four have steel girders or steel troughing and the remainder are arched. One of the overbridges has cast iron girders and the remainder steel girders. There are no viaducts or tunnels and the culverts are unimportant. All the works seem to be satisfactorily constructed: the girders have sufficient theoretical strength and those under the line gave moderate deflections under test.

CAMBRIAN COLLIERY. [WORKMENS TRAIN]233C. HE

Cambrian Colliery miners and a family group pose for the camera in front of the colliers' train at Clydach Vale in the early years of the 20th century.

John Ryan Collection/J.A. Peden

Tonyrefail station, looking towards Penygraig *c.* 1910, with the goods yard and signal box just visible beyond the platforms. *Lens of Sutton*

There are no public level crossings.

There are two new stations on the line, viz: Tonyrefail and Penygraig, the former being situated at 4 miles 33.7 chains from the commencement of the line and the latter at its termination.

Both stations have up and down platforms 350 feet long and 3 feet high. At each place ample accommodation is provided on the up platform, while on the down platform there are shelters or waiting sheds. At Penygraig there is a footbridge between the platforms.

The signal boxes etc on the new line are:

(1) Llantrisant Common Junction, containing 15 levers, of which 13 are now in use and two are spare;

(2) Gellyrhaidd Junction, containing 41 levers, of which 33 are now in use 8 are spare. This is the junction with the single line mineral branch to Hendreforgan. It would have been desirable, owing to the gradient, to have laid in runaway catch points on the Ely Valley line above the junction, but this was not found to be possible. Runaway catch points are, however, to be laid in below the junction, and the company should be requested to report when this has been done;

(3) Billups Siding, containing 13 levers, of which 9 are in use and 4 are spare;

(4) Tonyrefail Station, containing 25 levers of which 19 are in use and 6 are spare. The down starting signal at this place requires to be moved back nearer the signal box;

(5) Cilely Junction Box, containing 25 levers, of which 20 are in use and 5 are spare. Runaway catch points are required here on the down line, a short distance ahead of the down starting signal of the Tonyrefail Box;

(6) Dinas Isha Box, containing 21 levers, of which 17 are in use and 4 are spare. Runaway catch points have been ordered to be laid in on the down main line, and the company should be requested to report when this has been done;

(7) Naval Sidings Box, containing 21 levers, of which 16 are in use and 5 are spare;

(8) Penygraig Station Box, containing 33 levers, of which 26 are in use and 7 are spare.

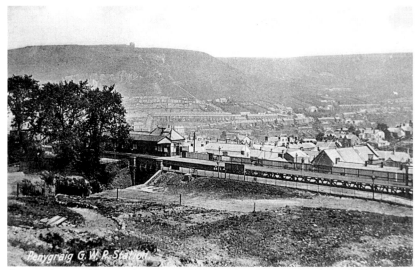

A general view of Penygraig station *c.* 1910 showing the extensive timber built building on the up platform and the platform extension of the same material.

Author's Collection (courtesy R.H. Marrows)

Colonel Yorke found the interlocking, in all cases, to be correct and the signalling arrangements satisfactory. He thus was able to recommend that the Board of Trade sanction the use of the line for passenger traffic, subject to the rectification of certain minor defects, identified in his report.

Two points should be made concerning Colonel Yorke's report: firstly, where he talks of the 'main line' near Mwyndy (Junction) signal box, he is, of course, referring to the line between Llantrisant station and Maesaraul Junction used by TVR passenger trains; and, secondly, it will be noted that the EVR followed conventional railway practice with the 'up' line being that in the direction of London (i.e. via Llantrisant), unlike neighbouring local railway companies, where 'up' was 'up the valley' and 'down' was 'down to the sea'.

The report of inspection for the section between Cowbridge Road Crossing (on the Mwyndy branch), Mwyndy Junction and Llantrisant was completed on 25th May, 1901. Colonel Yorke found the works and signalling arrangements here to be satisfactory, apart from some minor defects, and recommended that they be approved, the conditional sanction the Board of Trade being conveyed to the GWR on 30th May, 1901.

Chapter Six

Under the Great Western

The scale of works required for the doubling of the line and the introduction of the passenger train service drew attention to the somewhat anomalous position of the EVR, then still only leased by the GWR. The railway above Penrhiwfer was, of course, already owned by the latter company. An attempt to amalgamate the EVR with the GWR had been made in the 1871 Parliamentary Session, but this had come to nothing. Now, with the completion of the various improvements and the opening of the line to passengers in May 1901, the time clearly was ripe for a another move in this direction.

On 3rd July, 1902 the GWR Board heard that the Chairman of the EVR, Mr G.C. Williams, had enquired about the possibility of the undertaking being acquired by the larger company, and that the outline of such an arrangement had been discussed. Having heard the details of this proposal, the GWR Directors agreed that these negotiations should be continued. In the event, these quickly proved fruitful and at the meeting of the GWR Board, on 9th October, 1902, it was decided to include in a Bill powers for the acquisition of the EVR. This was authorised by the GWR Act of 11th August, 1903, with the amalgamation being effective from 1st July of that year. Under the terms agreed, GWR stock was to be issued in exchange for that of the EVR.

Passenger traffic on the Ely Valley line soon lived up to expectations, with ticket sales in 1903 amounting to 42,300 at Penygraig and 45,702 at Tonyrefail, representing daily averages of 135 and 145 respectively. By 1913 business had increased dramatically with 248,385 tickets (794 per day) being sold at Penygraig and 125,906 (402 per day) at Tonyrefail. Penygraig station was convenient for a wide urban area, which was not particularly well-served by the nearest TVR stations at Dinas and Llwynypia. After having receiving numerous petitions over the years, the TVR eventually bowed to public pressure and, on 9th March, 1908, opened a new station, called 'Tonypandy and Trealaw', midway between the two stations referred to above. The GWR, on the other hand, made no attempt to extend its Ely Valley passenger service beyond Penygraig to Clydach Vale.

The years up to the outbreak of World War I also saw a substantial increase in the volume of the coal traffic passing over the Ely Valley line, with the sinking of a new colliery at Coed Ely, roughly midway between Gellyrhaidd and Llantrisant Common Junctions, in 1906-1909, together with increased output from other mines served by the railway. As a result, the tonnage of coal forwarded increased from 928,602 tons in 1903 to 1,494,522 tons in 1913. The Cambrian Colliery at Clydach Vale, in particular, sent much of its output via the GWR route, rather than by the Pwllyrhebog branch of the TVR. So much so that in November 1912 Ammon Beasley, the TVR General Manager, was instructed by his Traffic Committee to try to secure a 'fair share' of the Cambrian Colliery traffic for the company. The output of the mines in the vicinity of Gilfach Goch, much of which passed over the Gellyrhaidd branch, also grew significantly during this period.

An early view of the Welsh Navigation Colliery, Coed Ely, served by the Ely Valley line and midway between Llantrisant Common Junction and Gellyrhaidd Junction.
Author's Collection (courtesy R.H. Marrows)

A later view of the Welsh Navigation Colliery, looking across the Ely Valley from Coed Ely.
Author's Collection (courtesy R.H. Marrows)

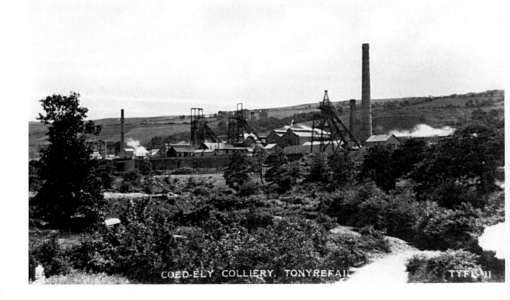

LLANTRISANT AND PENYGRAIG.											
Down Trains.	**Week Days only.**						**Up Trains.**	**Week Days only.**				
	a.m	p.m	p.m	p.m	p.m			a.m	a.m	p.m	p.m	p.m
Llantrisant .... dep	8 35	12 14	3 28	5 42	8 50	...	Penygraig .... dep	7 40	10 10	2 40	5 0	6 40 ...
Tonyrefail .... „	8 49	12 28	3 42	5 56	9 4	.	Tonyrefail .... „	7 48	10 18	2 48	5 8	6 48
Penygraig .... arr	8 57	12 36	3 50	6 4	9 12	...	Llantrisant .... arr	8 0	10 30	3 0	5 20	7 0 ...

GWR Public Timetable, January-April 1902.

The opening of the nearby colliery, together with new housing development in the area, led to repeated requests for a passenger station to be provided to serve the growing settlement of Coed Ely, about 2 miles south of Tonyrefail. This question was being raised even before the completion of Coed Ely Colliery. On 3rd June, 1908 the Surveyor to Llantrisant and Llantwit Fardre Rural District Council (L&LFRDC) informed his Members that he had met the GWR Divisional Superintendent, Mr Leaning, on the subject, which had also been raised by the colliery company.

The need for a station for Coed Ely was brought up again on a number of occasions, but it was not until 1915 that any real progress was made. On 8th July, 1915 the GWR Traffic Committee considered a proposal which had been made by the colliery owners, the Welsh Navigation Steam Coal Co. It was suggested that the GWR should construct the station and adjoining road overbridge, estimated to cost £3,500 and £2,100 respectively, with the colliery company contributing £1,500 towards the cost of the bridge, and forming the road approaches thereto. The Committee approved of this scheme, but only on condition that it await the cessation of hostilities or the emergence of other, more favourable circumstances. However, the colliery company was not willing to countenance such a delay, and on 29th July, 1915 the Traffic Committee heard that it had put forward a fresh proposal. It was now prepared to provide the necessary capital, which the GWR would then repay at £1,000 per annum, together with interest at 4½ per cent. This was agreed to and in the August edition of the GWR Magazine it was announced that a new station was to be built at Coed Ely.

The L&LFRDC, on the other hand, wished to see the new station built at Pantglas, about ½ mile down the valley. However, as this location was not acceptable to the colliery company, its offer to the GWR being dependent upon the station being located at Coed Ely, the Council was obliged to concede this point.

The war years and their immediate aftermath were not a good time to enter into commitments of this kind, however they might be financed, and in November 1919 the GWR informed the District Council that it could not, for the time being, proceed with the construction of Coed Ely station. This unfavourable climate persisted well into the post-war period, and it was not until November 1924 that the GWR Magazine was able to report that, as a consequence of 'industrial development' in the area between Llantrisant and Tonyrefail stations, it had been agreed to erect a new station. However, in place of the earlier location near Coed Ely Colliery, the station was now to be further up the line at Thomastown. The use of the name 'Thomastown', as suggested by the GWR, although geographically correct, was not to the liking of the District Council, but here the GWR proved more receptive. On 15th January, 1925 Members of the Council

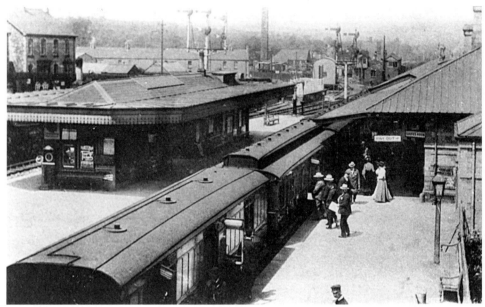

A Cardiff-bound stopping train stands in the up platform at Llantrisant station, *c.* 1910.
Lens of Sutton

A GWR 0-6-0ST hauls an up mineral train through Llantrisant station *c.* 1910.   *Lens of Sutton*

heard that the new station was to be called 'Coed Ely', which was accepted even though they would have preferred the Welsh form of 'Coed-lai'. Coed Ely station was opened to passengers only on 13th July, 1925.

The passenger train service on the Ely Valley line provided a good direct link between the settlements of the upper part of the Ely Valley and Llantrisant station, from where connections were available for Cardiff. However, as these mining communities, together with nearby Gilfach Goch, tended to look to the Rhondda Fawr for their shopping and other needs, the passenger railway, terminating as it did at Penygraig, some way short of this objective, was only of limited value for such purposes. As a result, alternative modes of transport were soon proposed to overcome this deficiency.

The first decade of this century saw the rapid growth of electric street tramways in the urban areas of South Wales. As early as 1901 the Parliamentary Committee of Glamorgan County Council had directed that notice be given for the promotion of a light railway, in the form of a street tramway, from Aberdare to Bridgend, via Maerdy, Porth, Tonyrefail, Blackmill and Tondu. Just how the trams would have coped with the fearsome gradients found on the inter-valley roads, however, remains unclear. The County Council had hoped that the application for a Light Railway Order could be made jointly with the district councils along the route, but the scheme met with opposition from L&LFRDC and was not taken any further.

A much more serious contender appeared with the formation of the 'Rhondda Tramways (RT) Co.' in April 1906, with the first routes opening on 11th July, 1908. On 5th November, 1908 the company introduced a service from Porth to Partridge Road, via Dinas, Penygraig and Tonypandy. This was followed, on 30th March, 1912, by a branch from Penygraig to Williamstown. Looking ahead, the tramways of the Rhondda Fawr were to be abandoned in favour of motor buses on 31st December, 1933, with the company changing its name to the 'Rhondda Transport Co.' in June 1934.

Although an extension of the tramway from Williamstown to Gilfach Goch, via Tonyrefail, was seen as a desirable objective, a cheaper, more flexible alternative was soon felt to be more appropriate. Under the Rhondda Tramways (Railless Traction) Act of 15th August, 1913 powers were obtained for a trolleybus route from the tramway terminus at Williamstown to Nicholl's Terrace, Gilfach Goch, passing via Tonyrefail and Gilfach station, and covering a distance of about 4¾ miles. The service, operated by six cars, each with a body made by the Brush Electrical Engineering Co. of Loughborough and mounted on a Daimler chassis, commenced on 22nd December, 1914. Unfortunately, the poor state of the roads, made worse by mining subsidence, played havoc with the cars and led to very high running costs. As a result, the trolleybus service was suspended from 11th March, 1915. Hopes were raised in 1919 that operations might be resumed, but to no avail, and the 'railless' cars were destined never to be re-introduced on the Williamstown-Gilfach Goch route.

LLANTRISANT AND PENYGRAIG & TONYPANDY. (Week Days only.)

	a.m.	a.m.	p.m.	p.m.	p.m.	p.m.	p.m.	p.m.	p.m.	p.m.	p.m.			a.m.	a.m.	p.m.	p.m.	p.m.	p.m.	p.m.	p.m.	p.m.	p.m.	p.m.
Llantrisant dep	8 37	11 32	12 32	2 15	3 30	5 40	5 50	7 42	10 17	10 50	11 45		Penygraig and											
Tonyrefail ,,	8 52	11 45	12 45	2 28	3 43	5 53	6 3	7 55	10 30	10 45	11 58		Tonypandy dep	7 45	10 5	12 30	1 40	2 50	5 2	6 50	8 50	9 15	11 15
Penygraig and													Tonyrefail ,,	7 52	10 12	12 37	1 47	2 57	5 12	6 57	8 57	9 32	11 22
Tonypandy arr	8 59	11 52	12 52	2 35	3 50	6 3	6 10	8 2	10 37	10 50	12 5 7		Llantrisant arr	8 3	10 22	12 47	1 57	3 7	5 22	7 7	9 8 7	9 32	11 35

5—Saturdays excepted. S—Saturdays only.

GWR Public Timetable 4th May to 11th July, 1914.

The main station buildings on the up platform at Tonyrefail, *c.* 1910.   *Lens of Sutton*

A view of Llantrisant station showing the extended facilities provided in connection with the opening of the line to Penygraig to passengers in 1901. The enormous nameboard carried the legend 'LLANTRISANT JUNCTION FOR TONYREFAIL & PENYGRAIG COWBRIDGE & TAFF VALE LINE'.   *Lens of Sutton*

As a replacement for the ill-fated trolleybuses L&LFRDC proposed an extension of the tramway from Williamstown to Gilfach Goch, and in July 1919 agreement was reached with RT Co. to seek a Light Railway Order for that purpose. Plans were deposited and notices published in November 1919, with the application to the Light Railway Commissioners being approved at the meeting of the District Council on 18th December. An inquiry into the proposal was held in Tonyrefail in March 1920, leading to the granting of the necessary order. However, apart from the Council agreeing, in September 1921, to apply for a loan for carrying out the work, little else was done, although the powers for building the tramway were kept alive until 1937.

South of Tonyrefail the railway enjoyed something approaching a monopoly as there was no direct road through this part of the Ely Valley. The ancient ridgeway from Tonyrefail to Llantrisant, involving some very steep climbs, was the only alternative available. As early as 11th September, 1901 the L&LFRDC had determined to make a new road through the valley, but it was not until 11th April, 1912 that the Council agreed to submit an application to the Roads Board for a grant towards the cost of construction. The Ely Valley Road, to give it its full title, was to consist of a number of sections of new highway, with use also being made of existing roads where these could be incorporated and upgraded to the appropriate standard. Work on the road started prior to World War I, but operations appear to have been suspended during the conflict, and it was not until 27th June, 1921 that work commenced on the completion of the road, with a total of 95 men being employed. Completed around the beginning of 1925, the Ely Valley Road provided a high standard route which ran, for most of its length, parallel to the railway through the valley. In October 1919 the District Council had decided to seek powers to construct a tramway along the new road, but had not taken matters any further.

The 1920s witnessed the rapid development of extensive networks of motor bus services throughout South Wales. The first example of significance in our area of interest was that to Clydach Vale, introduced by the RT Co. on 4th August, 1920. The following January the RT Co. began operating a bus service between the tram terminus at Williamstown and Gilfach Goch, providing, at last, a replacement for the defunct trolleybus route. The next important development came in May 1924 with the introduction, again by the RT Co., of a route between Porth, Tonyrefail and Coed Ely. This was followed, on 9th February, 1925, by a much bolder enterprise, a Porth-Tonyrefail-Cardiff service, with the RT Co.'s buses making use of the Ely Valley Road, south of Tonyrefail, in direct and highly effective competition with the railway. July 1925 saw the introduction of a Porth-Porthcawl service, while in 1927 the Tonyrefail-Cardiff route was extended to Treorchy, and Ferndale gained a through run to Porthcawl, operated by Rhondda Motor Services (later taken over by Red & White Services).

The Ely Valley Road joined that from Llantrisant to Pontyclun at Tonysguboriau (later Talbot Green), at a point near the Talbot Arms, about ½ mile to the west of the town of Llantrisant. A number of bus routes converged at this place and timetables were arranged so as to provide connections between the various services. However, it was not until 1938 that Rhondda Transport opened a proper bus station at Talbot Green, immediately adjoining the road junction, already referred to.

ELY VALLEY AND BROFISCIN BRANCHES. Week Days.

Distance		STATIONS.	Station No.	Gradient 1 in	Cardiff Empties 5.20 a.m. dep.	Engine dep.	Fontypr'd (Central) Passenger dep.	Passen'ger dep.	Fontypr'd (Central) Passenger dep.	Ffaldcaiach Ore dep.	Passenger dep.	Fontypr'd (Central) Passenger dep.
M.	C.				A.M.	A.M.	A.M.	A.M.	A.M.	A.M.	A.M.	A.M.
—	68	Peterston	2716		6 50	7 0	7 15	7 50	7 53	7 55	8 22	8 30
—	0	Llantrisant	2730	102 R	7 0		7 17		7 55	8 2		8 32
1	44	Mwrgydy Junction	2744	141 F			7 19		7 57			8 34
1	52	Cowbridge Road	2745									
1	62	Maesaraul Junc.	2746									
1	68	Maesaraul Sidg.	2747									
2	44	Bute Siding	2748	145 R								
2	36	Dowlais Co. Sid.	2749	120 R								
—	—	Soula Siding	2750									
—	—	Brofiscin	2751									
2	36	Common Junction		72 R				8 2				
3	1	Coed Ely Colly. Box	2753	87 R	7 15						8 30	
3	3	Coed Ely	2754	69 R	7 30						8 40	
4	30	Gallythaidd Junc.	2755	69 R	7 40	7 20					3 27	
6	4	Hendreforgan	2824	42 R						Z 3		
5	3	Tonyrefail	2756	50 R					7 51			
5	43	Coorlan Siding	2757	60 R								
5	58	Cilely Siding	2758	50 R								
6	70	Naval Siding	2760	40 R								
7	28	Penygraig	2761	120 F								
7	70	Nantgwyn Siding	2762	220 R								
7	48	Clydach Vale	2763	32 R								

Note: Tonyrefail arr. 8.36 a.m.; Engine to work 7.37 a.m. Penygraig Passenger.

Time Allowance for Ordinary Freight Trains — Point to Point Times / Allow for Stop / Allow for Start (Mins.)

Single Line worked by — Dell and Wooden Train Staff / Electric Train Staff / Wooden Train Staff.

Double Line / Crossing Stations / Train Staff Stations — Cowbridge Road Crossing, Maesaraul Junction; Penygraig, Gellyrhaidd Junction.

GWR Service Timetable, 12th September, 1928.

ELY VALLEY AND BROFISCIN BRANCHES.—Week Days—*continued.*

DOWN TRAINS. WEEK DAYS.

STATIONS.	Passenger (B) dep. a.m.	Goods dep. a.m.	Goods arr. a.m.	Goods dep. a.m.	Empties dep. a.m.	Pontyp'dd (Central) Passenger (B) dep. a.m.	Coke Ovens Goods dep. a.m.	Passenger (B) dep. a.m.	Passenger dep. p.m.	Pontyp'dd (Central) Passenger (B) dep. p.m.	11.35 a.m. Cardiff Empties dep.	Pontyp'dd (Central) Passenger (B) dep. p.m.	Passenger (B) dep. p.m.
Peterston						10 30	10 5	11 0	12 45	12 55	12 48	2 5	2 20
Llantrisant	9 25	9 30		9 40							1 2		
Mwyndy Junction						10 32				12 57	1 40	2 7	
Cowbridge Road		CR											
Maesaraul Junction		CR				10 34	10 12			12 59		2 9	
Maesarnul Siding		CR											
Bute Siding		CR											
Downis Co.'s Siding		CR											
Sculls Siding													
Brofiscin		10 10											
Common Junction			10 15	10 30									
Coed Ely Colliery													
Coed Ely	9 33		10 35	11 20				11 8	12 53		1 55		2 28
Gellyrhaidd Junction													
Hendreforgan					9 30								
Tonyrefail	9 40		11 25	12 30	9 40			11 15	1 0		2 5		2 35
Caerlan Siding													
Cilely Siding			12350	W12‖45									
Naval Siding													
Penygraig	9 47		12‖00				X 2	11 22	1 7				2 42
Nantgwyn Siding													
Clydach Vale													

Notes:
- Goods: Engine from shed 9.10 a.m. — Ynysmaerdy Colliery 9 50 10.5
- Empties: Second Trip of 6.30 a.m. ex Llantrisant.

GWR Service Timetable, 12th September, 1928.

ELY VALLEY AND BROFISCIN BRANCHES.—Week Days—*continued.*

DOWN TRAINS—WEEK DAYS.

STATIONS.	Pontyp'dd (Central) Passenger B dep.	Passenger B dep.	Llantwit Goods OS dep.	Passenger XS B dep.	Pontyp'dd (Central) Passenger B dep.	Fiald-caiach Iron Ore F dep.	Passenger B dep.	Pontyp'dd (Central) Passenger B dep.	Passenger B dep.	Coke Ovens Goods dep.	Pontyp'dd (Central) Passenger dep.	Passenger OS B dep.	Passenger Th.FSO B dep.
	P.M.	P.M.	P.M.	P.M.	P.M.	P.M.	P.M.	P.M.	P.M.	P.M.	P.M.	P.M.	P.M.
Peterston	3 57	4 5		5 22	5 30	5 40	6 5	7 28	7 59	8 0	9 18	9 35	10 35
Llantrisant	3 59				5 34			7 30		8 4	9 20		
Mwyndy Junction													
Cowbridge Rd.													
Maesaraul Jct.	4 1					5 50		7 32		8 10	9 22		
Maesaraul Sdg										X14			
Bute Siding													
DowlaisCo's. S.													
Sculls Siding													
Brofiscin													
Common Junction										SUSPENDED			
Coed Ely Colliery													
Coed Ely		4 13		6 30			6 13		8 3			9 45	10 45
Gellyrhaidd Junc.													
Hendreforgan													
Tonyrefail		4 20		5 36			6 20 T		8 10			9 50	10 50
Gwalia Siding													
Cilely Siding													
Naval Siding													
Penygraig		4 27					6 27 T		8 17 T			9 57	10 57
Nantgwyn Siding													
Clydach Vale													

T Three minutes extra allowed at Tonyrefail for collection of tickets on Saturdays.

GWR Service Timetable, 12th September, 1928.

ELY VALLEY AND BROFISOIN BRANCHES.—Week Days—continued.

UP TRAINS—WEEK DAYS

Distance M.C.	STATIONS	Station No.	Gradient 1 in	Point to Point Times Mins.	Allow for stop Mins.	Allow for start Mins.	Pontypridd (Cent.) Pass. 7.3 a.m. arr. B	Passenger dep. B	Cowbridge Passenger dep. B	Coke Ovens 5.30 a.m. Goods dep. B	Pontypridd (Cent.) Pass. 8.30 a.m. dep. B	Cardiff Cnal. arr.	Cardiff Cnal. dep.	Passenger dep.	Pontypridd (Cent.) Pass. 10.3 a.m. dep.	Goods dep.
—	Clydach Vale	2783														
1 28	Nantgwyn Siding	2782														
2 0	Penygraig	2781						7 37				8 55 / 9 15 P / 9 30	8 50 / 9 10 / 9 20 / 9 45	10 0		
2 35	Naval Siding	2780							8 10							
2 71	Stop Board	—														
3 50	Cilely Siding	2758														
3 65	Caerlan Siding	2757														
4 25	Tonyrefail	2756						7 44						10 7		
0 19	Hendreforgan Stop Board	2894														
4 78	Gellyrhaidd Jct.	—							8 14					10 11		
	Coed Ely	2755						7 48								
0 37	CoedEly Colly. Box	2754														
0 72	Common Junction	2753										9 35				
0 52	Brofiscin	2751														10 20 CR
	Sculls Siding	2750														CR
1 3	DowlaisCo's Sdg	2749														CR
1 14	Bute Siding	2748														CR
4 44	Maesaraul Sidg.	2747														
1 72	Maesaraul Jct.	2746				7 29			8 29	8 56					
	Cowbridge Road	2745													10 29	
8 56	Mwyndy Junction	2744				7 31	7 56	8 22	8 34	8 56	10 10	10 11	10 19	10 31	
9 28	Llantrisant	2720				7 34			8 37	9 0				10 33	10 45
	Peterston arr.	2716						X 2		X 2					

ELY VALLEY AND BROFISCIN BRANCHES.—Week Days—continued.

UP TRAINS WEEK DAYS. STATIONS.	Passenger dep. A.M.	Pontypridd (Cent.) Pass. 11.46 a.m. arr. P.M.	Passenger dep. P.M.	Fochriw Empties 11.0 a.m. dep. P.M.	Passenger dep. P.M.	Pontypridd (Cent.) Pass. 1.41 p.m. dep. P.M.	Goods arr. P.M.	Goods dep. P.M.	Pontypridd (Cent.) Pass. 3.3 p.m. dep. P.M.	Passenger dep. P.M.	Cardiff Coal dep. P.M.	Passenger dep. P.M.	Llantwit Goods 4.51 p.m. dep. P.M.	Pontypridd (Cent.) Pass. 5.15 p.m. dep. P.M.	Passenger SX dep. P.M.
Clydach Vale	10 55														
Nantgwyn Siding															
Penygraig			12 10		1 15					3 25	8 35	4 50			5 45
Naval Siding															
Stop Board							OW	1 0					SO		
Gilfai Siding							11 5	1 30							
Caerlan Siding			12 17		1 22					3 32		4 57			
Tonyrefail	11 2				1 26					3 36	3 46	5 1			
Heoldreforgan Stop Board															
Gellyrhaidd Jnct.							1 35	1 50							
Coed Ely	11 6		12 21				1 55	2 14							
Coed Ely Colly.															
Common Jnct.											Return of 11.35 a.m. Cardiff				
Brofiscin							Llantrisant								
Sculla Siding				1 21			Return of 9.40 a.m.						5 10		
D'w'l'is Co.'s Sg.													5 13	6 44	
Bute Siding															
Maesaraul Sid.															
Maesaraul Jn.		12 13				2 7			3 29						
Cowbridge Rd.				1 38											
Mwyndy Jnct.		12 14				2 9			3 31					6 46	
Llantrisant	11 14	12 16	12 29		1 32	2 10	2 30		3 33	3 44	4 6	5 9	5 18	5 48	5 58
Peterston arr.															

GWR Service Timetable, 12th September, 1928.

ELY VALLEY AND BROFISCIN BRANCHES—continued.

Up Trains.

Week Days.

STATIONS.	Goods. Ovens. Coke. 4.40 p.m. dep.	Pontypridd (Central) Pass. 6.33 p.m. dep.	Pass. dep.	Pontypridd (Central) Pass. 8.31 p.m. dep.	Passenger FSO arr.	Passenger FSO dep.	Pass. Th.SO dep.	Pontypridd (Central) Pass. 10.15 p.m. dep.	Ffaldcaiach Empties. 8.25 p.m. dep.
	P.M.	P.M.	P.M.	P.M.	P.M.	P.M.	P.M.	P.M.	P.M.
Clydach Vale...									
Nantgwyn Siding									
Penygraig	SUSPENDED		7 0			8 50	10 6		
Naval Siding ...									
Stop Board ...			7 7			8 57	10 15		
Cliffy Siding ...					8 56				
Coedfan Siding									
Tonyrefail ...			7 11			9 1	10 17		
Hendreforgan					9 0				
Stop Board									
Gellyrhaidd Junc.									
Coed Ely ...									
Coed Ely Colliery									
Common Junction									
Brofiscin ...									
Smills Siding ...									
Downais Co. Sid.									
Bnts Siding ...				8 57				10 42	
Maesmaul S'dg	6 44	7 2		8 59			10 25	10 44	11 2
Maesmaul Jct.	6 48	7 4		9 1				10 46	
Cowbridge Rd.	7 0	7 6	7 19			9 9			
Mwyndy Junct. ...		7 7							
Llantrisant arr.	X 14				9 9				11 10
Peterston arr.									

GWR Service Timetable, 12th September, 1928.

The popularity of the competing bus services had a dramatic effect on the passenger traffic of the Ely Valley line. The first station to suffer was Tonyrefail, where the number of tickets sold declined from nearly 126,000 in 1913 (402 per day), to only 21,825 in 1923 (70 per day), probably reflecting the success of the bus service between Williamstown, Tonyrefail and Gilfach Goch, introduced in January 1921. The opening of the Ely Valley Road and the further development of the bus network also led to a steep decline in passenger traffic at Penygraig during the 1920s. Tickets sold at this station had declined from nearly 250,000 in 1913 (794 per day) to 197,597 in 1923 (631 per day), but by 1930 the total for the year was down to only 20,765 (66 per day). At first sight, Tonyrefail experienced something of a recovery towards the end of this period, with the total number of tickets sold in 1930 rising to just over 30,000 (96 per day), but, by this date, returns from this station also included tickets sold at Coed Ely station. The above figures exclude season tickets, which showed similar rates of decline during this period. The passenger business at the Ely Valley stations remained at these greatly reduced levels throughout the 1930s.

The economic decline which set in after the General Strike of 1926 also depressed the railway's traffic, both in terms of numbers of passengers and the tonnages of goods and minerals carried. The volume of coal passing over the line fell, with the most significant losses resulting from the abandonment of the former Naval group of collieries at Penygraig, where the private siding agreements were terminated in 1931. This was followed, albeit on a smaller scale, by the closure of Caerlan Colliery, near Tonyrefail, in the mid-1930s.

Local goods traffic over shorter distances was also susceptible to competition from road hauliers, and declined considerably. The railway company itself transferred smaller consignments to the 'Railhead Distribution Scheme', whereby lorries were used to connect the railhead (in this case Cardiff) with the surrounding district. One such railhead delivery route took in Coed Ely, Tonyrefail, Gilfach Goch and Penygraig, en route between Llantrisant and Tonypandy.

Livestock had been quite an important item, with a total of 958 wagons handled in 1903, mostly at Penygraig. In 1923 the annual total of wagons dealt with at the branch stations was down to 534, but this declined dramatically during the inter-war period.

Away from the Ely Valley line, the Blackmill-Hendreforgan-Gilfach passenger train service was especially vulnerable to bus competition. Gilfach station was poorly sited, the trains were infrequent, and journeys involved time-consuming reversals at Hendreforgan and delays awaiting connections at Blackmill. It was not altogether unexpected, therefore, when the Gilfach service was suspended on 5th March, 1928. However, at this stage, the GWR did not intend to abandon this district entirely.

Over the years a number of attempts had been made to persuade the railway company to run passenger trains over the freight-only section between Hendreforgan and Gellyrhaidd Junction, but without success. A service bridging this gap, albeit provided by buses, had appeared to be in prospect on 22nd September, 1927, when the Cardiff Divisional Superintendent, F.G. Wainwright attended a meeting of the L&LFRDC, seeking licences for three 'AEC' buses to ply for hire between Gilfach Goch and Tonyrefail, in connection with Llantrisant-

Penygraig trains. This request was acceded to, but only on condition that the train service between Gilfach and Blackmill continued to run. As the GWR had in mind replacing the train with a Tonyrefail-Gilfach Goch-Blackmill bus route, this proviso clearly was not going to prove acceptable to the company.

Thus, on 13th October, 1927, F.G. Wainwright returned to the District Council to ask for the offending condition to be deleted. He explained that it was intended to offer through bookings on the new bus service and arrange connections with the trains at Tonyrefail and Blackmill stations, and that rail excursions would continue to be run from Gilfach station. These assurances appeared to have satisfied the Councillors as it was agreed to comply with Mr Wainwright's request.

However, the following March, when the Gilfach train service was withdrawn, there was a public outcry, with the district councils leading the way. Faced with this opposition, the GWR quickly relented, the train service being restored on 26th March, 1928. In what appears to have been a somewhat belated gesture towards local feelings, Gilfach station was renamed 'Gilfach Goch' on 30th June of that year. Prospects for the re-instated trains were not good, however, and, almost inevitably, permanent withdrawal of the service followed on 22nd September, 1930. This time the protests were more muted, with L&LFRDC restraining itself to a request for a substitute bus service to be provided. Unfortunately, by this date the GWR was no longer able to supply such a service, the company having transferred its bus interests to the Western Welsh Omnibus Co., which had been established on 1st April, 1929.

The line closures which took place during the inter-war years involved goods-only branches which had either become redundant as a result of the Grouping of 1922, or had seen very little traffic for some time. In 1930/31 the ex-TVR Common branch was closed as a through route, with a short section of line, to the west of Treferig Junction, being lifted in late 1931. However, just over a mile of track on this branch, running eastwards from Llantrisant Common Junction, was retained for wagon storage until 1st July, 1951. The former Ogmore Valley Railway line from Hendreforgan to Blackmill also ended its days in this fashion, with all coal from the Gilfach Goch area being brought out via Gellyrhaidd Junction and the Ely Valley line.

The first section of the former EVR to close, since the demise of the Castellau branch in 1867, was that between Mwyndy siding and Brofiscin on the Mwyndy branch, where the track was removed in November 1936. Formal abandonment of this section was sanctioned under the GWR Act of 10th June, 1937.

Passenger traffic on the Ely Valley line experienced a significant upturn during the war years, as a result of petrol rationing and restrictions on road transport. However, much of this additional traffic had fallen away by the time the branch became part of the Western Region of British Railways on 1st January, 1948.

158	LLANTRISANT AND PENYGRAIG.												
Miles					**Week Days only—One class only.**								
		a.m.|a.m.|a.m.	a.m.|p.m.	p.m.	p.m.	p.m.|p.m.|p.m.	p.m.	p.m.	p.m.
—	Llantrisant ...... dep	6 50| 8 18| 9 23	...|10 55|12 50	1 33	...| 2 20|...	D 0¼E 10| 6 5	...	7 55	...| 9N57| ...|10N35|...
4	Coed Ely .... ,,	6 59| 8 26| 9 32	...|11 3|12 58	1 41	...| 2 28|...	4D 8|4E18| 6 13	...	8 3	...| 9N45| ...|10N45|...
5	Tonyrefail .... ,,	7 5| 8 34| 9 36	...|11 9| 1 3	1 46	...| 2 33|...	4D15|4E25| 6 18	...	8 8	...| 9N50| ...|10N48|...
7¾	Penygraig .... arr	7 11| 8 43| 9 44	...|11 19| 1 11	1 54	...| 2 41|...	4D21|4E31| 6 20	...	8 10	...| 9N58| ...|10N56|...
		a.m.|a.m.	a.m.	p.m.	p.m.	p.m.|p.m.	p.m.	p.m.	p.m.
	Penygraig .... dep	7 40|10 0	...|10 50	...|12 20	1 12	...| 1 55| 3 23| 4 55|...	6 65	...| 8 48	...| 9N59| ...|11N10|...
	Tonyrefail .... ,,	7 45|10 5	...|10 55	...|12 25	1 17	...| 1 59| 3 28| 5 0|...	7 0	...| 8 53	...|10N 4| ...|11N16|...
	Coed Ely ... ... ,,	7 48|10 8	...|10 58	...|12 28	1 20	...| 2 2| 3 31| 5 3|...	7 3	...| 8 56	...|10N 7| ...|11N19|...
	Llantrisant . ... .. arr	7 56|10 16	...|11 6	...|12 36	1 28	...| 2 10| 3 39| 5 11|...	7 11	...| 9 4	...|10N15| ...|11N27|...

GWR Public Timetable 3rd July, 1939 to 24th September, 1939.

Llantrisant drivers Fred Harwood and George Wilks pose in front of '14XX' class 0-4-2T No.
1471 at that station on 20th May, 1950.   *Ian L. Wright*

Chapter Seven

Decline and Fall

The years after Nationalisation were a period of progressive decline for the railways of the upper Ely Valley, leading to the gradual abandonment of the network originally formed by the EVR and the E&CVR, together with the various connecting lines. There were some brighter moments, usually resulting from investment decisions by fellow nationalised industry, the National Coal Board, but these turned out to be transitory in nature.

Local passenger traffic fell sharply after the end of the war, and from 1951, one by one, the branch line services radiating from Llantrisant station were withdrawn. The first to go was that to Cowbridge, on 26th November, 1951. This was followed, on 31st March, 1952, by the passenger trains to Pontypridd, which passed over the Mwyndy branch to Maesaraul Junction in order to reach the ex-TVR line to Treforest. With the drastic reduction of its service in the Winter timetable of 1953, the Ely Valley line looked set to follow in quick succession. However, it was not until the Spring of 1958 that formal closure proposals were put forward.

These were considered by the Transport Users' Consultative Committee for Wales and Monmouthshire in a report made public on 10th April, 1958. Objections to the closure had been lodged by the Clerk to Llantrisant & Llantwit Fardre Rural District Council and a deputation from the Ely and Rhondda Valleys. The Committee found that the withdrawal of the passenger service would save at least £8,100 per annum and that very few people were using the trains compared with the parallel bus routes. It concluded:

The bus has superseded the train in public favour in this area so that the branch line service has become superfluous and a liability the Transport Commission should no longer bear.

Notices were posted shortly afterwards announcing the intention to close the line to passengers from 9th June, 1958. The notice itself also outlined the alternative bus services provided in the area by Rhondda Transport and Red & White Services, which, it must be admitted, were far more extensive than the dismal four trains each way which, by this time, passed for the railway timetable. Parcels were to continue to be handled at Tonyrefail, with Tonypandy station on the Rhondda Fawr branch catering for the needs of the Penygraig area.

The date for the withdrawal of the Llantrisant-Penygraig passenger trains coincided with the start of the Summer timetable, although full details of the service itself were still included in the published document! As there was no Sunday service, the last trains ran on Saturday, 7th June.

The final day of the timetabled service was a very quiet affair with a single auto-trailer sufficing for the traffic on offer. The trains saw a few extra passengers, including railway enthusiasts and local people. At 8.30 pm the auto-train pulled out of Penygraig to the blast of detonators and made its way down the valley for the last time, witnessed by small groups of people at the terminus and stations along the route.

A Stephenson Locomotive Society excursion, consisting of two ex-Taff Vale Railway auto-trailers and 0-6-0PT No. 6423, stands in the Penygraig bay at Llantrisant on 12th July, 1952.

R.C. Riley

0-6-0PT No. 6423 propels a Stephenson Locomotive Society special consisting of a pair of ex-Taff Vale Railway auto-trailers to the start of the single line section to the east of Cowbridge Road Crossing on 12th July, 1952. *S. Rickard Collection/Copyright B.J. Miller*

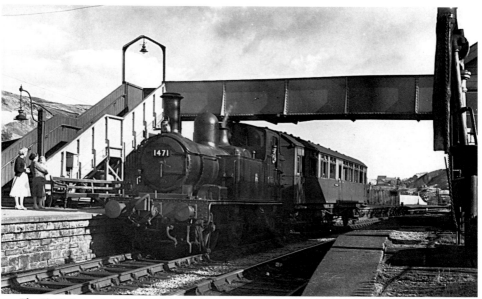

The Ely Valley auto-train, consisting of No. 1471 and a Diagram A9 auto-trailer (converted from a steam railcar), at Penygraig in September 1954. *D. Chaplin*

Class '55XX' 2-6-2T No. 5574 with a Stephenson Locomotive Society special on the down main line at Llantrisant on 13th July, 1957. This train subsequently worked over the Ely Valley line as far as Gellyrhaidd Junction and from there to Britannic Colliery above Gilfach Goch. *S. Rickard Collection/Copyright B.J. Miller*

The coaches for the Ely Valley passenger service, with a diagram A44 auto-trailer nearest the camera, in the Penygraig bay at Llantrisant, *c. 1957.*   *Author's Collection*

A wet winter's day at Penygraig on 4th January, 1958 as No. 1471 and trailer maintain their solitary vigil before returning to Llantrisant.   *H.C. Casserley*

BRITISH RAILWAYS (WESTERN REGION)

PUBLIC NOTICE

The British Transport Commission hereby give notice that on and from Monday, 9th June, 1958, the passenger train service operating between Llantrisant and Penygraig will be withdrawn and the following stations closed for passenger traffic:-

COED ELY   TONYREFAIL   PENYGRAIG

Road services are operated in the area by the Rhondda Transport Company Limited and the Red and White Services Limited.

Collection and Delivery arrangements for parcels traffic and Passengers' Luggage in Advance will continue to be available throughout the area.

Facilities for the handing in and/or collection of parcels by the public will be available at Tonyrefail; the nearest Station to Penygraig offering this facility will be Tonypandy.

Any further information required can be obtained upon application to:-

Mr. H. S. Jenkins,
District Commercial Manager,
Cardiff.
Tel. No.: Cardiff 21021 Extn. 434

Station Master, Llantrisant.
Tel. No.: Pontyclun 234
Station Master, Tonyrefail.
Tel. No.: Tonyrefail 3
Station Master, Tonypandy.
Tel. No.: Tonypandy 2216

K. W. C. GRAND,
General Manager

Paddington.
April, 1958

PRINTED BY THE CARDIFF HERALD PRINTING PRESS LTD.

Table 133		LLANTRISANT and PENYGRAIG

WEEK DAYS ONLY—(Second class only)

Miles		am	am	pm S	pm	pm	pm S											
	Llantrisant — — dep	7 0 ..	8 20 ..	1 10 ..	4 55 ..	5 45 ..	7 55 ..	..	..	..	..	..	..	..	..	..	..
4	Coed Ely	7 10 ...	8 30	1 20	5 5	5 55	8 5	..	..	..	..	..	..	..	..	..	..
5	Tonyrefail — — ..	7 20 ...	8 36 ..	1 25 ..	5 10	6 0 ..	8 10 ..	..	..	..	..	..	..	..	..	..	..
7¼	Penygraig .... arr	7 28	8 44	1 32	5 17	6 7	8 17	..	..	..	..	..	..	..	..	..	..

Miles		am	am	pm S	pm	pm	pm S											
	Penygraig — — dep	7 45 ..	8 46 ..	1 45 ..	5 20 ..	6 30 ..	8 30 ..	..	..	..	..	..	..	..	..	..	..
2¼	Tonyrefail	7 50 ...	8 51	1 50	5 25	6 35	8 35	..	..	..	..	..	..	..	..	..	..
3¼	Coed Ely .. — —	7 53 ...	8 54	1 53	5 28 ..	6 38 ..	8 38	..	..	..	..	..	..	..	..	..	..
7¼	Llantrisant.............. arr	8 1	9 2	2 1	5 36	6 46	8 46	..	..	..	..	..	..	..	..	..	..

S Saturdays only

The final passenger service timetable before closure, commencing 16th September, 1957.

No. 1471 and auto-trailer in the bay at Llantrisant ready to form the 4.55 pm to Penygraig on the last day of service, Saturday 7th June, 1958.   *S. Rickard Collection/Copyright B.J. Miller*

Penygraig station on 7th June, 1958, with No. 1471 and trailer in the up platform.   *John Hodge*

No. 1471 attracts attention from young and old at Penygraig on 7th June, 1958.   *John Hodge*

A Stephenson Locomotive Society special consisting of '64XX' 0-6-0PT No. 6416 sandwiched between three auto-trailers at Penygraig on 2nd July, 1960. Little had changed since the withdrawal of the passenger service just over two years earlier.

Revd J. Parker/Hugh Davies Collection

The SLS excursion waits near Mwyndy Junction while '64XX' 0-6-0PT No. 6416 obtains refreshment on 2nd July, 1960.   *Revd J. Parker/Hugh Davies Collection*

This apparent lack of interest may be explained by the fact that the following day, a Sunday, saw the running of a final excursion from Penygraig to Porthcawl. This produced crowded scenes at Penygraig and the intermediate stations as many people sought to combine the joys of a day at the seaside with the experience of a last trip over the Ely Valley line.

Following the closure of the ex-TVR Pwllyrhebog branch on 1st July, 1951, the output of the Cambrian Colliery at Clydach Vale had been concentrated on the Ely Valley route, significantly boosting its traffic. Elsewhere, however, traffic was lost as the result of the closure of other collieries directly or indirectly connected to the Ely Valley line. Cil Ely Colliery had closed on 14th October, 1950, followed by the Trane and Llewelyn Pits near Gilfach Goch in 1953. In 1957 a connecting tunnel was opened between Coed Ely and Cwm Colliery, near Beddau and served by the ex-TVR line from Maesaraul Junction to Treforest, and from 1966 all of Coed Ely's coal was brought to the surface this way. This development deprived the Ely Valley line of the output of the Coed Ely Colliery, but resulted in the unusual sight of coal being hauled up the valley for processing at the adjoining coke ovens. Coke was available for outward traffic, but this also proved attractive to road transport.

The first significant line closure since Nationalisation came on 5th June, 1961 with the abandonment of the line to Gilfach Goch, following the demise of Britannic Colliery, near its terminus, on 30th June, 1960. The branch, which included the whole of the former Ely Valley Extension Railway, together with the Gellyrhaidd branch of the EVR, was then secured out of use on 9th March, 1962, with the exception of a short section of line at Gellyrhaidd Junction which was retained for stabling banking engines until 1st March, 1964.

'The Leek' excursion, organised by the Monmouthshire and West Glamorgan Railway Societies and hauled by '56XX' 0-6-2T No. 6614, pauses for water at Llantrisant yard on 27th June, 1964. *John Dore Dennis Collection*

Class '37' Co-Co No. 37 255 stands in Llantrisant yard after arriving with a stone train from Creigiau Quarry, via Common Branch Junction and Maesaraul Junction, on 4th April, 1974.
M.R.C. Price

Class '37' Co-Co No. 37 287 propels its van over Cowbridge Road Crossing *en route* from Llantrisant yard to Cwm Colliery on 10th May, 1982.   *R.W. Ranson*

The reduction in train movements following the withdrawal of the passenger service and the closure of the various collieries meant that the double track section between Mwyndy Junction and Penygraig could no longer be justified. The section above Gellyrhaidd Junction was singled on 9th September, 1963, with that southwards to Mwyndy Junction following on 3rd October, 1965. A crossing loop was then created at Gellyrhaidd Junction. The former up line was retained in use above this point, while to the south of the crossing place sections of both up and down lines were used. At the same time the short length of double line on the Mwyndy branch, in the vicinity of Cowbridge Road Crossing signal box, was also singled.

This period also saw the closure of the remaining goods stations on the Ely Valley line. That at Tonyrefail went on 7th October, 1963, with the sidings being removed during the following January, while Penygraig goods yard was closed on 12th October, 1964.

After the withdrawal of the last of its branch line passenger train services in 1958, Llantrisant station continued in use for the various stopping trains which ran along the South Wales main line between Cardiff and Bridgend. However, in March 1963 the station was listed for closure to passengers, with the publication of 'The Reshaping of British Railways' (otherwise known as the 'Beeching Report'): this took place on 2nd November, 1964. The goods yard then continued in use for another 20 years, with the last loaded coal wagon being deposited in the yard on 1st November, 1983 and removed empty three days later.

Ex-British Railways class '03' 0-6-0 diesel shunter, then owned by British Coal, at Coed Ely on 17th June, 1982. *R.W. Ranson*

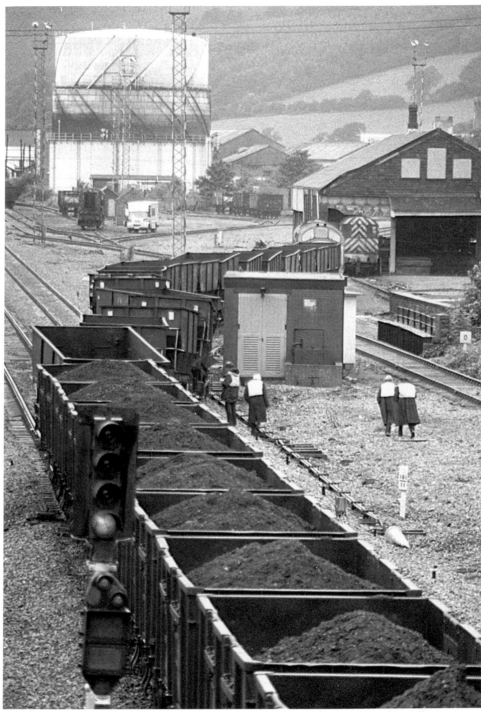

The 2.30 am Severn Tunnel Junction-Llantrisant blocks the South Wales main line following a derailment of some of its wagons on 23rd June, 1982. *R.W. Ranson*

Class '37' No. 37 305 and brake van at the site of Llantrisant Common Junction on the Ely Valley line, 17th June, 1982.   *R.W. Ranson*

The surviving railway network was dealt a severe blow with the closure, on 31st March, 1967, of the Cambrian Colliery at Clydach Vale. With the loss of this important source of traffic the line above Coed Ely Colliery was closed completely on 2nd April, 1967, with the section from that colliery to Mwyndy Junction then being downgraded to the status of a siding. Track lifting above Coed Ely was completed in August 1967. The section of the Mwyndy branch, from Maesaraul Junction to the I.C.I. explosives depot at its terminus, followed on 7th October, 1968. The rest of this branch, from Maesaraul Junction to Mwyndy Junction, was retained in use as part of the route to Cwm Colliery.

This greatly reduced system was to remain in place for a further 15 years, until the closure of first the coke ovens at Coed Ely and then Cwm Colliery, deprived the surviving railways of their last remaining sources of traffic. The last revenue-earning train left Coed Ely on 4th October, 1983, the branch being spiked out of use on 21st February, 1984. However, the line was then brought back into use for a final enthusiasts' excursion on 31st March, 1984, before being permanently secured out of use on 2nd April, 1984. Track was lifted in March and August 1989, with the points at Mwyndy Junction being removed on 14th June, 1990.

The ex-EVR line from Mwyndy Junction to Maesaraul Junction, together with the last remnant of the former Llantrissant & Taff Vale Junction Railway, also succumbed following the closure of Cwm Colliery in 1987. The last mineral train from Cwm worked over this section on 2nd March, 1987, although here too it was followed by an enthusiasts' railtour which ran as far as the colliery siding on 11th April of that year. The line was taken out of use in October 1989 beyond a stop block which had been erected at a point immediately to the east of Cowbridge Road level crossing, about 15 chains from the junction with the South Wales main line.

The final passenger working over the last remaining section of the Ely Valley line, an excursion organised by the Monmouthshire Railway Society, in front of the coke ovens at Coed Ely on 31st March, 1984.

B.J. Ashworth

The final enthusiasts' working, organised by the Monmouthshire Railway Society, approaching the site of Coed Ely station on the Ely Valley line on 31st March, 1984.   *M.J. Back*

Bearing the headboard 'Coed Ely Coupling', the final excursion passes Mwyndy Junction on 31st March, 1984.   *M.J. Back*

Class '37' No. 37 109 brings a train of ballast hoppers across the Talbot Green bypass on the diverted branch to Cwm on 3rd March, 1993.   *M.J. Back*

The new level crossing over the Talbot Green by-pass on the diverted Llantrisant-Cwm line in 1995.   *Bill John*

Chapter Eight

Locomotive and Train Working

At the time of its promotion in 1856 very little thought appears to have been given to the question of motive power to be used on the EVR. It was not until 7th February, 1860 that the company's Managing Director, Richard Bassett, was instructed to make enquiries for the purchase of a second-hand broad gauge engine with which to work the line. He was not successful in this quest, but fortunately the arrangement entered into with the GWR later that year provided the necessary means for working the traffic of the railway.

The GWR locomotive *Alligator,* an 0-6-0 goods engine built in 1848, is recorded as allocated to Llantrisant in July 1862. However, at this date there does not appear to have been a shed as such at Llantrisant and it is doubtful whether one existed during the broad gauge period. A plan of the station, dated 4th May, 1863, shows no evidence of even the most basic of facilities for the locomotive department.

No other details have come to light of broad gauge engines employed on the EVR prior to gauge conversion in 1872, but it is interesting to note that four years later, in April 1876, the GWR sold broad gauge 4-4-0ST *Corsair* to Cilely Colliery for use as a stationary engine.

The construction of an engine shed at Llantrisant was authorised by the GWR Board on 3rd January, 1872, in the wake of the decision to abandon the broad gauge in South Wales. The new depot was sited on the up side of the EVR, close to the junction with the South Wales main line. The facilities included a two-road stone-built shed about 90 feet long, with a large water tank and a small turntable, accessed, rather inconveniently, from one of the shed roads.

With the substantial growth in traffic on the EVR towards the end of the century, the facilities provided at Llantrisant in 1873 became increasingly inadequate. As a result, construction of a new locomotive depot was authorised by the GWR Board on 26th March, 1896. The old engine shed was closed in October 1900, being replaced by a three-road building of standard 'Dean' design. This was of stone construction, about 120 feet long, with a north-light roof, and was located to the north of the site of the old shed. A new combined locomotive coal stage and water tank, and a larger turntable were also provided. The new facilities were to last, in more or less this form, until the end of steam in 1964.

The allocation at Llantrisant Shed in January 1902 consisted of a mixture of classes '1016', '1076', '1854' and '2721', all 0-6-0STs. Other engines included a '57' class 0-6-0 No. 67, originally built in 1856, and a 'River' class 2-4-0 No.73.

Engines of the 'Aberdare' class of 2-6-0 had first appeared at Llantrisant in 1901 for working long distance coal traffic to Swindon. None were there in 1906, but in January 1910 Nos. 2625 and 2651 were recorded. By this date the '1076' and '2721' engines were the predominant type of 0-6-0ST at the shed, with five of each class being present, together with two '1016s' and three '1854s'. From 1910 engines of these classes were progressively fitted with pannier tanks.

The 'Aberdares' had gone for good by 1914, with ex-R.O.D. 2-8-0s being used in their place in 1921. 'Dean' and 'Standard class 0-6-0s were also present at this time.

The combined loco coal stage and water tank with its steeply graded approach at Llantrisant.
The wagons in the background belong to Welsh Navigation Steam Coal Co., owners of Coed Ely
Colliery.   *B. Roberts Collection/J.A. Peden*

A quiet scene at Llantrisant Shed, on 9th July, 1950, with a '42XX' 2-8-0T at the coal stage and
two 0-6-0PTs parked in a siding on the left.   *R.K. Blencoe Collection*

A workmen's train service was established on the Ely Valley line prior to the introduction of ordinary passenger trains in 1901. On 18th November, 1896 the GWR Traffic Committee accepted an application from the Cambrian Navigation Collieries Co. for such a train to be run between Penygraig and Clydach Vale for the benefit of its workmen, with a platform for this purpose being provided adjoining the colliery at Clydach Vale.

The Llantrisant-Penygraig passenger train service, introduced in May 1901, consisted of five trains each way, except on Sundays. Trains were made up of four- and six-wheeled low-roofed coaches, hauled by 0-6-0STs of the '1076' and '2021' classes. The coaching stock was stabled overnight at Penygraig, with the engine running light from and to Llantrisant Shed at the beginning and end of each day.

On 1st July, 1904 two additional return workings were added to the timetable, one in the early afternoon, on Thursdays and Saturdays only, and the other in the late evening, on Saturdays only. The passenger service was gradually improved over the years leading up to World War I, as more people used the railway, to a pre-war peak, from 1st February, 1913, of eight trains each way, Mondays-Saturdays. This required the use of two train sets. Despite its popularity, however, the line did not attract a Sunday service.

The Ely Valley line also proved popular as a route for excursion traffic, especially to Porthcawl. The TVR had run such trains, via Pontypridd and Maesaraul Junction, but this journey was rather circuitous for passengers from the Tonypandy-Penygraig district. However, TVR trains did have the advantage of being able to use the Cowbridge bay at Llantrisant for reversal *en route* to Porthcawl and other destinations to the west of the station. The GWR, on the other hand, was obliged to reverse its trains on the busy South Wales main line. It was necessary, at first, for returning trains to be shunted from the up platform road onto the down main line, before being reversed to the down platform, as it was not possible to depart for Penygraig (or for the TVR route for that matter, in which case trains had to be shunted across to the Cowbridge bay) from the up main line. It was during one of these manoeuvres, on 7th October, 1901, that a GWR excursion train returning from Swansea to Penygraig was propelled into a siding, colliding with some wagons in the process. On this occasion the fault was found to lie with the signalman, who was reduced in grade and deprived of his bonus. However, this incident may have been influential in the decision of the GWR Traffic Committee, on 22nd January, 1902, to install a connection, complete with facing point lock, between the up main and down branch lines at Llantrisant. This enabled trains to depart for Penygraig directly from the up main line platform.

The war years saw a significant reduction in the passenger train service, with the need to conserve men and materials for the war effort being paramount. There was also an conscious attempt on the part of the authorities to curtail demand, which had grown considerably during this period, by reducing frequencies and raising fares. By November 1918 the Llantrisant-Penygraig timetable was down to only six trains each way daily, requiring the use of only one train set.

It was not until the introduction of the Summer timetable in July 1921 that the line regained its pre-war standard of eight trains each way, with two train sets again being employed. In the following Summer the number of trains was

Llantrisant Shed, looking towards Penygraig on 5th May, 1951, with two '57XX' 0-6-0PTs and a '14XX' 0-4-2T 'on 'shed'.   *H.C. Casserley*

A class '42XX' 2-8-0T and two class '57XX' 0-6-0PTs outside the shed at Llantrisant, while another 0-6-0PT stands alongside the coal stage on 6th November, 1957.
Industrial Railway Society/Brian Webb Collection

increased to nine each way, but this proved to be a temporary extravagance, as the following Winter saw the service back to eight trains each way. The branch timetable then remained in this basic form throughout the 1920s.

Many children from Tonyrefail and Coed Ely travelled daily by train to Cowbridge, the boys to attend the Grammar School and the girls the High School, but the railway timetable did not accord well with the school day. There was also the change of trains at Llantrisant, in both directions, to contend with. After many requests and complaints from the local authorities and others, the GWR arranged for a direct service to be run between Tonyrefail and Cowbridge. This change, which is recorded in the Winter timetable introduced on 24th September, 1928, was made possible by extending two Cowbridge-Llantrisant workings, one in the morning and the other in the afternoon, through to Tonyrefail, at times convenient for the school day. The school train, which was auto-worked from September 1930, was known to its regular clientele as 'Emma', its two coaches being used to enforce a rigid apartheid between the sexes. Following the opening of a new school at Tonyrefail in 1934, the need for through working faded away and the school trains made their last appearance on the Ely Valley line in the Winter timetable introduced in September 1935. However, 'Emma' continued to run between Llantrisant and Cowbridge.

With the start of the Summer timetable in July 1930 the Ely Valley line became the first of the three Llantrisant branch line services to go over to auto-working. Initially, the auto-coaches were stabled at Penygraig in the customary fashion, with the engine running light in each direction at the beginning and end of the working day. However, this proved only a temporary arrangement, as in the following year the auto-trailers were transferred to Llantrisant. This resulted in the addition of a passenger train in each direction, in place of the light engine workings, bringing the daily total for the service up to nine trains each way.

The first auto-fitted engines to be shedded at Llantrisant were of the '517' 0-4-2T, 'Metro' 2-4-0T and '1076' 0-6-0T classes, but it was the 'Metros' that were to become the mainstay of the auto-train turns at the shed. Of this class, No. 3584 was at Llantrisant from 1934 to 1945 and No. 3586 from 1936 to 1938 and from 1943 to 1949. No. 3586, together with sister engine No. 3594, which had arrived at Llantrisant in 1940, were the mainstay of the Penygraig service during the war years. On 24th April, 1936 the then new '48XX' class 0-4-2T No. 4871 (No. 1471 from 16th November, 1946) arrived at the shed, where it was used on the Cowbridge and Pontypridd lines before becoming the usual motive power on the Ely Valley line auto-trains. Auto-fitted '64XX' 0-6-0PT engines also made brief appearances at Llantrisant in the late 1930s and after World War II.

Excursion trains continued to be popular and after 1931 a new route became available with the opening of the connecting link between the South Wales main line and the former Penarth Railway at Leckwith, between Ely and Cardiff General stations. This enabled trains to run direct from the Ely Valley line and Llantrisant to Penarth and Barry Island for the seaside, and to Ninian Park Platform for association football. Nevertheless, Porthcawl retained its place as a favourite destination for excursions from the branch to the coast. One beneficial effect of the 'Grouping' in 1922 was that such trains could now make use of the Cowbridge bay at Llantrisant, where reversal could take place clear

A Ninian Park-Penygraig return football special hauled by a '57XX' class 0-6-0PT gets a clear road for the Ely Valley line at Llantrisant in September 1954.   *D. Chaplin*

No. 1471 and trailer wait for custom in the Penygraig bay at Llantrisant station *c.* 1958.
David Lawrence/Hugh Davies Collection

of the main line, before proceeding to Porthcawl. When not in use the stock used on these trains was stabled alongside the locomotive depot at Llantrisant.

As we have seen, goods and mineral workings on the former EVR lines had long been the preserve of older 0-6-0Ts of the '1076', '1854' and '2721' classes. In 1921 engines of the first of these classes had dominated, with no less than 10 being shedded at Llantrisant. The 1920s saw their gradual displacement by those of the '1854' and '2721' classes. This was followed, from March 1929 onwards, by the arrival of the new class '57XX' 0-6-0PTs, with the last class '2721' engine going in 1939, followed by the final '1854' in 1942.

Class '56XX' 0-6-2T engines, shedded at Abercynon from 1925, appeared on goods and mineral workings from the former TVR system, passing over ex-EVR metals from Maesaraul Junction, but were not based at Llantrisant, except for short periods when the usual class '57XX' and '42XX' locomotives were shopped.

Class '42XX' 2-8-0T locomotives were shedded at Llantrisant for main line workings, but were also permitted to work Llanharry-Dowlais iron ore trains via Maesaraul Junction, Pontypridd and Nelson to Ffaldcaiach on the former Taff Bargoed Joint Line. This traffic came to an end in 1930, with the cessation of iron production at Dowlais, and, henceforth, iron ore trains were confined to the South Wales main line. The 2-8-0Ts also made occasional forays up the ex-EVR lines conveying the Llantrisant breakdown crane to rescue derailed wagons. In 1938 five members of this class were at Llantrisant: Nos. 4200, 4208, 4252, 4288 and 5235.

The wartime emergency timetable, brought in on 25th September, 1939, saw the Penygraig passenger service cut back to seven trains each way. It then fluctuated between seven and eight trains each way, during the war years, with single train working, which had been introduced with the emergency timetable, remaining in force from then on.

The war years also saw the running of a number of munitions' workers trains, via Llantrisant, to the ordnance factory at Tremains, east of Bridgend. Three shifts were served - morning, afternoon and evening - with trains running from and returning to Merthyr, Treherbert, Maerdy and Penygraig. The first three services ran via Pontypridd and Maesaraul Junction, reversing in the Cowbridge bay at Llantrisant station on the down journey. The Penygraig service, which also reversed in this manner, was worked by a Llantrisant engine and crew, with a five-coach non-corridor set, which was stabled in the up sidings near Mwyndy Junction, running empty to and from Penygraig at the beginning and end of each turn. These trains were usually in the hands of 0-6-0PT No. 3656 which had arrived new at Llantrisant in January 1940. There was also a service from Gilfach Goch to Tremains, but this ran via Tondu and Bridgend and was worked by Tondu engines and crews.

With the end of hostilities the Llantrisant-Penygraig timetable was improved to a new peak of 12 trains each way, by the end of 1946.

Apart from a brief reduction to eight trains each way in 1947 resulting from the coal shortage which followed the severe winter of 1946/47, this pattern was to remain in place until the end of the Summer service in September 1949. The subsequent Winter timetable saw the start of the progressive decline in the number of workings on the Ely Valley line, with two round trips being withdrawn. The service was cut back again, to eight trains each way, in the

0-6-2T No. 5618 holds up the traffic at Cowbridge Road Crossing with the 11.00 am Llantrisant -Pontypridd Coke Ovens goods on 3rd May, 1958.

S. Rickard Collection/Copyright B.J. Miller

Class '42XX' 2-8-0T No. 4222 outside Llantrisant Shed on 5th October, 1964.

S. Rickard Collection/Copyright B.W. Miller

Summer timetable of June 1951, and then to six in September of that year. Finally, in the Winter timetable, introduced on 21st September, 1953, two trains, a midday working and another in the late evening, became Saturdays only. This severely limited the usefulness of the train service, as on Mondays-Fridays there was not a train over the branch between the 8.46 am ex-Penygraig and the 5.40 pm return from Llantrisant.

For a short period prior to the withdrawal of the Llantrisant-Cowbridge passenger service in November 1951, ex-GWR diesel railcar No. 18, used on that line, was also employed on two round trips on the Ely Valley line, leaving Llantrisant at 12.45 pm and 4.45 pm and returning from Penygraig at 1.10 pm and 5.10 pm. Both workings were labelled 'Limited accommodation' in the public timetable.

Apart from this minor intrusion, class '14XX' 0-4-2T No. 1471 continued to provide the usual form of motive power on the Ely Valley passenger trains. Sister engine No. 1421 arrived at Llantrisant in December 1949, replacing 'Metro' 2-4-0T No. 3586, but was mainly used on the Pontypridd service until that was withdrawn in 1952. Locomotives of the '57XX' class of 0-6-0PTs could also be seen at various times, hauling ordinary compartment coaches in place of the usual auto-trailer.

Following the withdrawal of the Llantrisant-Penygraig service in 1958, No.1471 was transferred to Exeter Shed to work the Exe Valley line, before being condemned on 15th October, 1963 (by which time it had accumulated a total mileage of 690,345), and cut up at Swindon the following month.

Auto-trailers converted from GWR steam railcars were used on the Ely Valley line for many years, before being replaced by compartment brake-thirds of Diagram A44, which had been converted to auto-working in 1955. In the final year of the service one of the open trailers of Diagram A27, built in 1928, was employed. Latterly a single car sufficed on most branch workings, but even then two trailers were sometimes required, especially in the summer months when fine weather encouraged many of the inhabitants of the upper part of the Ely Valley to take trips to the seaside at Porthcawl. The following auto-trailers were recorded on the Ely Valley line or at Llantrisant after 1950:

Date	No.	Diagram	Source	Built/converted	Condemned
1950	11	A9	Ex-steam railcar	1919	1951
1950	1090	Ex-Rhymney Railway	Third*	1920	1958
1951	103	Z	Ex-steam railcar	1915	1953
1951	106	A6	Ex-steam railcar	1917	1952
1951	107	A7	Ex-steam railcar	1916	1952
1951	108	A7	Ex-steam railcar	1916	1954
1951	114	A9	Ex-steam railcar	1919	1955
1951	125	A10	Ex-steam railcar	1920	1953
1951	4303	Ex-Barry Rly		1914	1951
1952	22	J1	Bristol C. & W. Co.	1906	1956
1952	100	Z	Ex-steam railcar	1915	1955
1953	1067	Ex-Rhymney Railway	Third*	1920	1957
1957	255	A44	Ex brake third	1955	1963
1958	159	A27	Swindon	1928	1963

* intermediate auto-coach used for strengthening purposes

The Cowbridge branch ex-GWR diesel railcar No. 22 and its crew at Penygraig on one of its two daily workings north of Llantrisant in 1951. The scale of the accommodation then provided at the station is clearly apparent in this view.   *R.C. Riley*

A Diagram A44 trailer and crew at the up platform at Penygraig, *c.* 1957.
David Lawrence/Hugh Davies Collection

Excursion trains from the Ely Valley line made use of a set of non-corridor coaches which was kept at Llantrisant for that purpose. These trains often required the services of two 0-6-0T engines to cope with the severe gradients on the upper part of the branch. The usual pattern was for trains to run to Cardiff for rugby or soccer matches on Saturdays in the season, and to Porthcawl or Barry Island in the summer months. When the traffic for a football match was not expected to justify the running of an excursion train, an extra train, usually made up of two coaches, was run from Penygraig to Llantrisant to connect with a main line working to Cardiff. As excursion trains had continued to run on other South Wales lines after the withdrawal of their regular passenger services, it came as something of a shock to the inhabitants of the upper part of the Ely Valley when they discovered that this was not to be the case on their branch line.

A number of steam-hauled excursions, organised by various enthusiasts' societies, also ran over the former EVR lines in the 1950s and early 1960s. On 13th July, 1957 one such tour, arranged by the Midland Area of the Stephenson Locomotive Society (SLS), ran up the Ely Valley line, as far as Gellyrhaidd Junction, before turning off for Gilfach Goch. The train, consisting of two auto-trailers hauled by class '55XX' 2-6-2T No. 5574, then returned to Mwyndy Junction, before reversing for the journey, via Maesaraul Junction, to Pontypridd.

Another excursion, once again arranged by the Midland Area of the SLS, ran through to Penygraig on 2nd July, 1960, and was made up of three auto-cars, hauled by class '64XX' 0-6-0T No. 6416. It is believed that this was the last steam-hauled passenger train to run over the Ely Valley line north of Mwyndy Junction.

The final steam-hauled passenger train to run over ex-EVR metals was 'The Leek', a six-coach special, conveying about 200 members of the Monmouthshire and West Glamorgan Railway Societies, on 27th June, 1964. This train, hauled by class '56XX' 0-6-2T No. 6614, passed over the section from Maesaraul Junction to Llantrisant station, *en route* from Pontypridd, before venturing, somewhat cautiously, down the Cowbridge branch.

After the withdrawal of the passenger train service in 1958 the Ely Valley lines became the preserve, to a very large extent, of class '57XX' 0-6-0Ts, with no less than 11 of these engines being recorded at Llantrisant in March 1959. Four class '42XX' 2-8-0Ts were retained for long-distance work. This regime remained in force until the arrival of English Electric type '3' (later class '37') Co-Co diesel-electric locomotives in August 1964. Llantrisant was closed as a steam shed the following October, giving way to a new diesel stabling point and train crew depot.

The Working timetable for April 1966, not long before the closure of the railway above Coed Ely, gave four return workings between Llantrisant yard and Clydach Vale, with two others as far as Coed Ely, all worked by type '3's, together with a 350 hp 0-6-0 diesel shunter (later class '08') working over the Mwyndy branch to the explosives depot at its terminus. Other trains also passed over this line as far as Maesaraul Junction, *en route* to Cwm Colliery and Creigiau Quarry on the ex-TVR lines.

LOCAL TRIP WORKING

LLANTRISANT H68
1750 HP DIESEL ELECTRIC (CANTON 813A)

			arr	dep	
Llantrisant S.P.	..	..		06||35	
Llantrisant	..	..		06 40	Daily
Cwm Colliery	..	..	07 00	07 50	
Llantrisant	..	..	08 25	09 05	
Cwm Colliery	..	..	09 25	10 05	
Llantrisant	..	..	10 40	11 20	SX
Creigiau Quarry	..	..	12 00	13 00	
Llantrisant	..	..	13 50	14 45	
Dowlais Works	..	..	16 10	17 20	SX
Llantrisant	..	..	19 25	19||35	
Llantrisant S.P.	..	..	19||40		
Llantrisant	..	..		22 35	SX
Barry	..	..	00 02	01 10	MX
Llantrisant	..	..	02 30	02||35	
Canton	..	..	03||00		
Llantrisant	..	..	10 40	11 20	Q SO
Cwm Colliery	..	..	11 45	12 45	
Llantrisant	..	..	13 25	13||30	
Llantrisant S.P.	..	..	13||35		

LLANTRISANT H69
1750 HP DIESEL ELECTRIC (CANTON 813B)

			arr	dep	
Canton Depot	..	..		05||40	MX
Llantrisant	..	..	06||10	06 15	Daily
Aberthaw	..	..	08 35	09 15	
Bridgend	..	..	10 10	10 42	
Llantrisant	..	..	11 10		
Llantrisant	..	..		14 30	SX
Cwm Colliery	..	..	14 55	15 35	
Llantrisant	..	..	16 15	16 55	
Cwm Colliery	..	..	17 20	18 00	
Llantrisant	..	..	18 40	19 20	SX
Cwm Colliery	..	..	19 45	20 25	
Llantrisant	..	..	21 05	23 40	SX
Severn Tunnel Jcn.	..	..	01 10	02 20	MX
Llantrisant	..	..	03 45		

LLANTRISANT J86
1750 HP DIESEL ELECTRIC (MARGAM 862A)

			arr	dep	
Llantrisant S.P.	..	..		05||20	Daily
Llantrisant	..	..	05||25	05 30	
Creigiau Quarry	..	..	06 10	07 10	
Llantrisant	..	..	07 50	08 30	SX
Coedely	..	..	08 50	09 10	
Llantrisant	..	..	09 30		
SHUNT.					
Llantrisant	..	..		11 25	
Coedely	..	..	11 45	12 00	
Gellyrhaidd	..	..	12 05	12 10	
Common	..	..	12 15	13 00	
Llantrisant	..	..	13 15	15 30	SX
Dowlais Works	..	..	16 45	17 50	
Llantrisant	..	..	19 25	00 45	MX
Margam (H. Yd.)	..	..	02 07	03 40	MX
Llantrisant	..	..	05 04		
Llantrisant	..	..	07 50	08 15	SO
Pengam Sdgs.	..	..	09 05	09 15	
Dowlais Works	..	..	09 30	10 50	
Pengam Sdgs.	..	..	11 05	11 15	
Leckwith	..	..	11 45	12 15	
Llantrisant	..	..	12 45	12||50	
Llantrisant S.P.	..	..	12||55		

LLANTRISANT J87
1750 HP DIESEL ELECTRIC (MARGAM 862B)

			arr	dep	
Llantrisant S.P.	..	..		06||05	
Llantrisant	..	..	06||10	06 15	SX
Clydach Vale	..	..	07 15	08 15	
Llantrisant	..	..	09 20	10 05	
Clydach Vale	..	..	11 05	12 05	
Llantrisant	..	..	13 10	13||45	
Llantrisant S.P.	..	..	13||50	16||05	
Llantrisant	..	..	16||10	16 15	
Clydach Vale	..	..	17 05	18 05	
Llantrisant	..	..	19 00	19 30	Q
Clydach Vale	..	..	20 25	21 00	
Llantrisant	..	..	21 55	22||00	
Llantrisant S.P.	..	..	21||05		
Llantrisant	..	..		06||30	SO
Llantrisant	..	..	06||35	06 40	Asst.
Cwm Colliery	..	..	07 05	07 55	Asst.
Llantrisant	..	..	08 35	08 50	
Coedely	..	..	09 10	09 30	
Llantrisant	..	..	09 40	10 20	
Coedely	..	..	10 40	11 00	
Gellyrhaidd	..	..	11 05	11 15	
Common	..	..	11 20	12 00	
Llantrisant	..	..	12 45	12||50	
Llantrisant S.P.	..	..	12||55		

LLANTRISANT T32
350 HP DIESEL SHUNTER (CANTON 701)

			arr	dep	
Llantrisant S.P.	..	..		05||55	Daily
Llantrisant Yard	..	..	06||00		
SHUNT.					
Llantrisant Yard	..	..		07 05	MX
Llanharry Quarry	..	..	07 17	07†35	
Llantrisant	..	..	07†45		
SHUNT.					
Llantrisant	..	..		10 10	Daily
Llanharry	..	..	10 17	10 40	
Llanharry	..	..	10 47	11 30	
Brofiscin	..	..	12 00	12 30	
Llantrisant	..	..	13 00	14 00	SX
Llanharry	..	..	14 12	14 40	
Llantrisant	..	..	14 57		
SHUNT.					
Llantrisant	..	..		21||50	
Llantrisant S.P.	..	..	21||55		
Llantrisant S.P.	..	..	13||00		SO

Extract from the BR (WR) Cardiff Division, Cardiff Valleys Local Freight Working Timetable, 18th April, 1966.

Class '37' No. 37 305 propels its brake van back to Llantrisant after leaving wagons at Coed Ely on 17th June, 1982. *R.W. Ranson*

Llantrisant goods shed with the Ely Valley line curving away to the right immediately beyond on 8th June, 1983. *Robert Darlaston*

In the May 1982 Working timetable there were four round trips between Llantrisant Yard and Coed Ely, with a further six workings each way to Cwm Colliery, all undertaken by class '37' locomotives.

The last inward coal train to Coed Ely Coke Ovens, on 29th September, 1983, was worked by class '37' Co-Co No. 37 222 with 15 hopper wagons. The final revenue working from the coke ovens, on 4th October, 1983, was in the hands of class '08' diesel shunter No. 08 350, hauling one loaded and four empty wagons. On the section between Maesaraul Junction and Llantrisant yard this sad duty was performed by Co-Co No. 37 244 on 2nd March, 1987.

No. 37 244 remained at Llantrisant until 9th March, the last engine to be stabled there. The final duty to be performed by a Llantrisant crew occurred on 13th March, when 11 parcels vans were moved from Cardiff to Llantrisant for storage. With its work at an end, the train crew depot was closed on 27th March, 1987.

A number of diesel multiple unit (dmu)-worked enthusiasts' railtours ran over the truncated network in its final years. Three excursions were of special note in that they provided the last passenger train workings over particular sections. On 14th May, 1977 the 'Midland Welshman' tour, organised by the Railway Correspondence and Travel Society and employing a class '120' cross country dmu, ran to Coed Ely and to Cwm Colliery, before forming the final passenger working over the surviving remnant of the ex L&TVJR Llantrisant No. 1 Railway to Creigiau Quarry. This followed hot on the heels of another excursion, organised by the Monmouthshire Railway Society (MRS), which had worked a similar itinerary on 26th March, 1977. The last enthusiasts' trains to run over the former EVR lines, following the end of revenue traffic, were the 'Coed Ely Coupling' to Coed Ely on 31st March, 1984, and the 'Tower Road Railtour' over the Mwyndy branch, *en route* to Cwm Colliery, on 11th April, 1987. Both trains were organised by the MRS using six-car class '117' dmus, the former being strengthened by a single-car unit.

Class '08' 0-6-0 diesel shunter No. 08 481, then on loan to British Coal, at Cowbridge Road Crossing *en route* from Cwm Colliery to Cardiff Canton diesel depot on 17th June, 1982.

R.W. Ranson

Chapter Nine

Along the Lines

This chapter takes the form of a tour, at somewhat indeterminate date, of the Ely Valley line and its branches, with historical details of the various locations included, as appropriate. Distances are given in miles and chains and are taken from the junction with the South Wales main line at Llantrisant, in the case of the main Ely Valley line, and from the junctions with the latter where the subsidiary branches are concerned. The journey from Llantrisant to Penygraig was, in railway parlance, via the down line with the return being by the up line. However, the terms 'upper' and 'lower', where used in this description, relate, more naturally, to the geography of the valleys.

Llantrisant-Clydach Vale

Llantrisant was one of the first batch of stations authorised by the Board of the South Wales Railway Company at its meeting on 29th April, 1850, although at this date the Directors were undecided as to whether to call it 'Llantrissant' or 'Cowbridge Road'.

The station, prior to the building of the EVR, was a simple wayside affair, with up and down platforms and a goods siding, off the up line, serving a goods shed and loading bank to the west of the passenger platform. A typical 'Brunellian' style station building was provided on the up platform, with a matching waiting shelter on the down.

The EVR originally joined the SWR, immediately to the west of that railway's bridge over the River Ely, by means of a trailing connection off the up line. Three loop sidings ran back from the EVR line, parallel to the SWR, with a connection from their western extremities to the down main line. When, in 1864, the standard gauge line was laid for the benefit of the Cowbridge Railway, it ran alongside the broad gauge EVR line from Mwyndy Junction, before crossing the SWR to reach the Cowbridge bay on the down side of the station.

The end of the broad gauge in 1872 was followed by a substantial improvement of the layout of the EVR lines at Llantrisant, authorised on 4th December, 1872. New up and down running lines were provided for a short distance on the branch, clear of the exchange sidings, and involving the resiting, nearer to Llantrisant station, of the junction with the South Wales main line. This junction was controlled by Llantrisant East signal box, with another box, known as 'Llantrisant Central', controlling certain yard connections. The new arrangements were approved by Colonel Rich on behalf of the Board of Trade on 23rd June, 1874.

The passenger facilities offered at Llantrisant remained largely unaltered after the arrival of the Cowbridge and Pontypridd services in 1865, despite the growth in traffic over the years. On 3rd January, 1883 the GWR Board considered a memorial from 'persons living in the district of Llantrissant

'County' class 4-6-0 No. 1027 *County of Stafford* brings an up mixed main line passenger and parcels train into Llantrisant station in 1951.   *R.C. Riley*

Llantrisant station with a class '56XX' 0-6-2T No. 6652 on an up mixed freight, *c.* 1963.

R. Mason

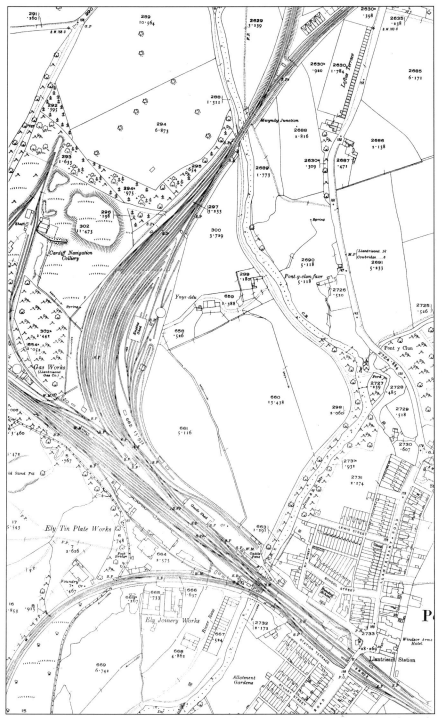

Llantrisant station to Mwyndy Junction, with the locomotive depot visible to the right of the extensive sidings on the Ely Valley line. *Reproduced from the 25", 1919 Ordnance Survey Map*

Tondu 2-6-2T No. 3100 calls at the down main platform at Llantrisant with a Cardiff-Bridgend return football excursion in September 1954.   *D. Chaplin*

Non auto-fitted 0-6-0PT No. 4674 departs for Penygraig from the bay platform at Llantrisant with a Diagram A44 auto-trailer on 13th July, 1957.   *S. Rickard Collection/Copyright B.J. Miller*

Station' asking for the station platforms to be raised and lengthened. Substantial alterations were approved on 26th March, 1888 and completed in 1891. These also gave considerably improved accommodation for TVR and interchange passengers.

Further major changes at the station were required to accommodate the passenger service to Penygraig. On 1st December, 1898 the GWR accepted the tender of A.E. Parfit for the new works. The old cramped goods yard was swept away, to be replaced by a greatly enlarged facility to the west of the River Ely. This enabled a new bay platform to be provided, complete with an almost full length canopy, on the up side of the station. Additional sidings and running lines were also added each side of the Ely Valley running lines, together with the new locomotive depot on the up side of the line, beyond the goods yard.

This layout survived largely unaltered until just after the withdrawal of the Ely Valley passenger service in 1958. In the final months of that year the Penygraig bay line was removed and the junction with the South Wales main line simplified. This junction was remodelled again in September 1968, with single lead connections to the Ely Valley line and the Cowbridge bay, each side of a facing crossover in the main line. The number of sidings in Llantrisant yard was gradually reduced in the years that followed. The station buildings and platforms were demolished not long after closure to passengers in 1964.

Beyond the station the Ely Valley line curved through almost 90 degrees, past the goods yard and locomotive depot, to Mwyndy Junction. Connected to the sidings on the down side of the line was the first colliery to be encountered on the branch - Lanelay (or Cardiff Navigation) Colliery. A mine had opened here at about the time of the promotion of the EVR and was connected to the railway by 1876. It suffered from poor geological conditions, and, as a result, passed through a variety of owners over the years, before being closed by the last of these, the Bargoed Coal Co., in November 1929. However, the private siding agreement was not terminated until 20th October, 1936, the siding itself being removed in 1938.

At Mwyndy Junction (0 m. 47 ch.) the Mwyndy branch parted company with the main Ely Valley line. The signal box (0 m. 43 ch.), on the up side of the line just before the junction, was brick-built with a hipped roof. It had opened in 1901, replacing the earlier box dating from 1874, which had been situated in the 'vee' between the main and branch lines. Mwyndy Junction signal box was closed on 9th March, 1969.

From just beyond Mwyndy Junction the Ely Valley line ran almost due north, for about a mile, to the site of the former Castellau branch junction, at mile post 1¾. For many years this section of the branch was an unspoilt rural interlude on the journey, but on 22nd December, 1921 a private siding agreement was entered into with the Powell Duffryn Steam Coal Co. for a temporary siding to serve its Llantrisant (or Ynysmaerdy) Colliery about to be sunk almost directly opposite the above mentioned milepost. This siding was opened on 28th February, 1922. Sinking of the new colliery also commenced in 1922 and was completed in 1926, but the new mine failed to live up to expectations and ceased production in 1933. Work on its reopening commenced in 1937, but a massive explosion on 2nd June, 1941 finally persuaded Powell Duffryn to abandon the attempt.

The view from the Penygraig auto-car, hauled by '14XX' 0-4-2T No. 1471, as it rounded the curve past Llantrisant yard, with its extensive siding accommodation on both sides of the running lines, on 24th May, 1958.   *Robert Darlaston*

0-6-0PT No.4674 (non auto-fitted) and trailer at Mwyndy Junction on a Llantrisant-Penygraig working on 13th July, 1957.   *S. Rickard Collection/Copyright B.J. Miller*

Mwyndy Junction and signal box on 6th May, 1961. The Ely Valley line is on the left and
the Mwyndy branch is on the right. *Michael Hale*

Up and down loop lines had been brought into use, in connection with this
colliery, on 15th December, 1924, with signal boxes provided at the two
extremities: Ynysmaerdy South (1 m. 30 ch.) and Ynysmaerdy North (2 m. 01
ch.) The North box was closed and its connections taken out of use on 2nd
September, 1956, with the South box and its connections following on 9th of that
month. A coal stacking site was later established on the up side of the line at
this point, with the connections from the up and down main lines being brought
into use on 8th May, 1960. They were taken out of use on 28th February, 1966,
then reinstated on 11th September, 1967, and finally abandoned on 8th July
1968.

From milepost 1¾ the line curved to the west, before bridging the River Ely
once more and arriving at Llantrisant Common Junction (2 m. 30 ch.). The
signal box here was replaced by a standard GWR design in 1924. This was
eventually closed on 3rd October, 1965.

Beyond Llantrisant Common Junction the railway continued its course tight
up against the western side of what, until 1906, had been another undeveloped
part of the Ely Valley. However, on 22nd September of that year an agreement
was entered into for a temporary siding to a new colliery being sunk on the
down side of the railway. The siding was brought into use on 17th June, 1906,
and sinking of the Navigation Steam Coal Co.'s Coed Ely Colliery was
completed in 1909. The new mine was to be an important source of traffic for
the railway for over 70 years, and was equipped, from the outset, with its own
coke ovens and by-products plant. The permanent siding arrangements,
reported to be ready for inspection on 22nd December, 1908, consisted of

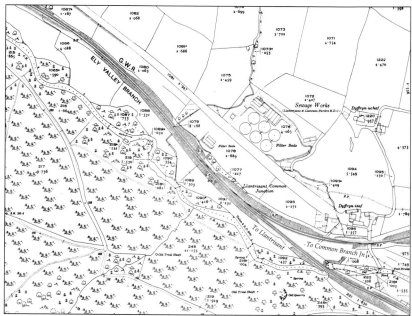

Llantrisant Common Junction. *Reproduced from the 25", 1920 Ordnance Survey Map*

trailing connections, to the up line at 3 m. 01 ch. and to the down at 3 m. 64 ch., with the lower junction being controlled by an 11-lever signal box (2 m. 75 ch.) and the upper by a ground frame. Coed Ely signal box was inspected by Colonel H.A. Yorke, who, in his report, dated 4th January, 1909, recommended that Board of Trade sanction be granted for the use of the new works.

In November 1911 Coed Ely Colliery was acquired by David Davis & Sons Ltd, which, in 1916, became part of the Cambrian Combine, this in turn becoming part of Welsh Associated Collieries Ltd in 1929. Finally, under an agreement dated 8th March, 1935, this concern was merged with the Powell Duffryn Steam Coal Co. to form Powell Duffryn Associated Collieries Ltd.

On 20th May, 1923 new sidings to the south of the colliery were brought into use, together with a new connection to the up line at Llantrisant Common Junction. Coed Ely signal box was closed and the old connection to the up line removed. Just below the upper junction a tramway crossed the railway by means of a girder bridge, construction of which had been approved by the GWR on 17th July, 1907, to convey coal from Tylcha Fach Colliery, on the up side of the line, to the Coed Ely Colliery sidings. The upper junction was taken out of use on 10th October, 1970, with the private siding agreement for the lower junction being terminated on 30th November, 1983.

Not far beyond the upper junction was Coed Ely station (4 m. 01 ch.), dating from 1925, and consisting of up and down platforms each 300 feet long. The main station building, on the up platform, was of a non-standard design,

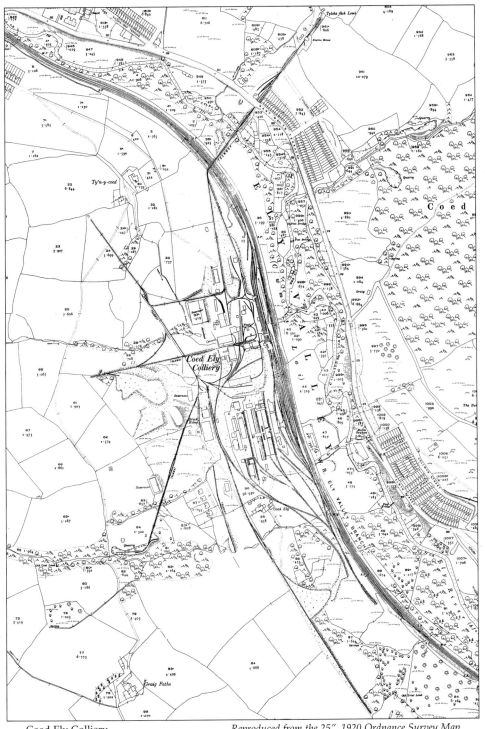

Coed Ely Colliery.

Reproduced from the 25″, 1920 Ordnance Survey Map

Coed Ely Colliery at the then terminus of the single track branch from Llantrisant on 8th June, 1983.   *Robert Darlaston*

A Llantrisant-Penygraig auto-train, propelled by the ubiquitous No. 1471, near Coed Ely on the last day of service, Saturday 7th June, 1958.   *John Hodge*

The view from the footbridge at Penygraig looking towards Tonyrefail in September 1954, with the Ely Valley auto-train hauled by No. 1471 coasting down the 1 in 120 gradient into the station.
D. Chaplin

The 5.20 pm Penygraig-Llantrisant calls at the up platform at Coed Ely station on 3rd August, 1957. On this occasion the usual engine, No. 1471, was away being overhauled and the train was made up of two non-corridor coaches, hauled by a '57XX' 0-6-0PT.   *Robert Darlaston*

Class '14XX' 0-4-2T No. 1471 propels the 5.15 pm Penygraig-Llantrisant auto-train at Coed Ely station in April 1956. The trailer is a Diagram A44 ex-brake third converted for this purpose in 1955.   *Robert Darlaston*

No. 1471 and a Diagram A27 auto-trailer forming the 5.20 pm Penygraig-Llantrisant at Coed Ely station on 5th April, 1958.   *Robert Darlaston*

crudely reminiscent of one of Brunel's station types, constructed of timber framing and asbestos sheeting and containing waiting rooms and toilets. A booking office was provided alongside the approach footpath from the main road, at the north end of the up platform. The down platform was without any form of shelter, and a footbridge was also lacking communication between the two platforms being by means of a sleeper crossing.

From Coed Ely station the line ran in a north-westerly direction, before bridging the River Ely for the fifth and final time and curving gently to westwards to Gellyrhaidd Junction (4 m. 24 ch.). Prior to the doubling of this section, the junction had consisted of a single turnout, with a loop siding on the Gellyrhaidd branch. A signal box had existed at Gellyrhaidd Junction from at least 1887, but this was replaced, at the time of the doubling in 1898, by a new box (4 m. 27 ch.), on the up side of the line. A down goods loop was later provided, avoiding the junction itself. The layout was simplified in later years, with the branch connection being taken out on 15th March, 1964. The signal box remained in use, however, first to control the entrance to the double line after the singling of the section above Gellyrhaidd Junction in 1963, and then the passing loop, which was formed when the line southwards to Mwyndy Junction was singled two years later. The box then continued in this role until the closure of the line above Coed Ely in 1967.

About a quarter of a mile north of Gellyrhaidd Junction had been a siding, serving Tydu Colliery on the up side of the line, which had been provided under an agreement, dated 2nd May, 1861, with the Ely Valley Coal Co. and T. Edmunds. This siding, which originally took the form of a loop off the single track main line, was disused by 1872. However, on 10th May, 1883 the GWR Board gave authority for it to be used by the contractor J.E. Billups, the Minute noting that the siding had 'never been altered from broad to narrow gauge.' Henceforth, it was always known as 'Billups Siding', even though it passed through various users over the years, with the agreement with the last of these, M.R. Rowlands, ending on 31st December, 1904. Billups Siding signal box, which had controlled the two siding connections, was finally removed in 1906.

Above this point the line continued on an embankment to Tonyrefail station (4 m. 77 ch.), situated immediately to the south of a bridge over the road to Blackmill. The passenger station, opened in May 1901, was equipped with stone-built station buildings of standard GWR design, with the booking office on the up side and a matching shelter on the down. The platforms were connected by ramps to the road below and there was no footbridge.

To the north of the underbridge on the up side of the line was the goods station. This facility had been authorised by the EVR on 2nd October, 1857, with the formation of a platform and the road approach being reported as complete on 11th June, 1860. The layout prior to doubling had consisted of a loop siding off the single track main line, serving a small goods shed and a short siding, with another siding added later. With the doubling of the line between Gellyrhaidd Junction and Cilely Junction in 1899, the arrangements were altered to provide connections to the sidings off the up and down lines, under the control of a new signal box (5 m. 12 ch.), called 'Tonyrefail Station'. On 22nd March, 1905 the GWR authorised the laying of an additional siding in the goods yard. In 1908 a single

Gellyrhaidd Junction, looking north on 20th September, 1962. The line on the left is the remnant of the former Gellyrhaidd branch to Hendreforgan which was retained for stabling engines used for banking trains up to Clydach Vale. Class '57XX' 0-6-0PT No. 9778 awaits its next task alongside the signal box.   *C.H.A. Townley*

Gellyrhaidd Junction and signal box, looking towards Llantrisant on 30th March, 1964. The connection to the former Gellyrhaidd branch on the right had been severed earlier in the month, but the box remained in use for main line purposes.   *Robert Darlaston*

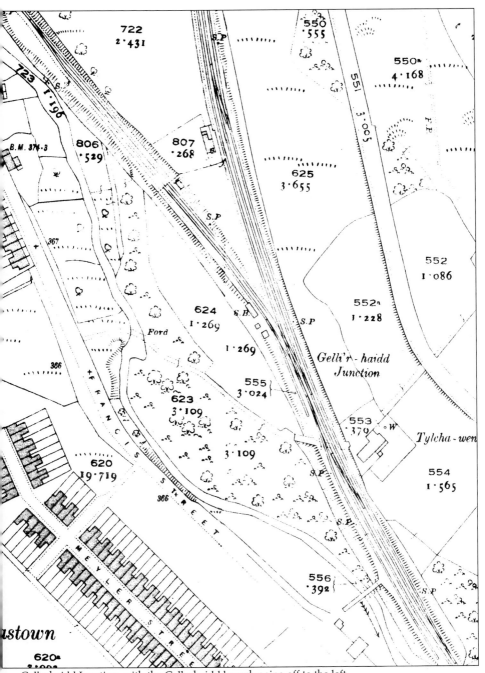

Gellyrhaidd Junction, with the Gellyrhaidd branch going off to the left.
Reproduced from the 25", 1919 Ordnance Survey Map

A general view of Tonyrefail in its pre-passenger service days, showing goods station to the left of the railway bridge.   *Graham Croad Collection*

Looking from the west towards Tonyrefail station, *c*. 1905, with the passenger accommodation on the right of the railway bridge and the goods yard to the left.   *Graham Croad Collection*

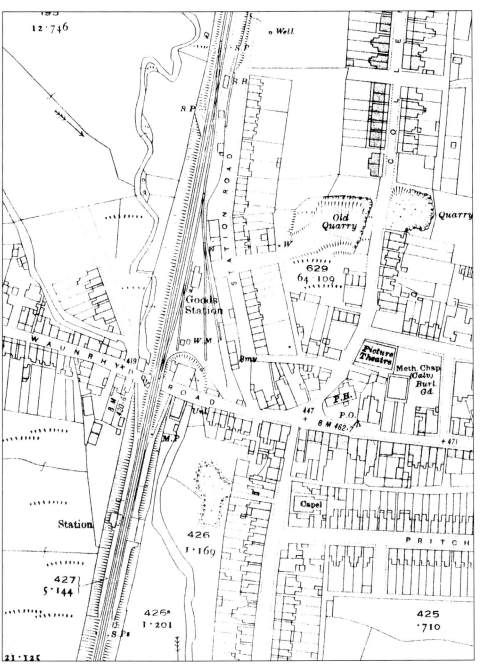

Tonyrefail station, with the passenger and goods facilities separated by Waunrhyd Road.
Reproduced from the 25″, 1919 Ordnance Survey Map

Tonyrefail, looking towards Penygraig on 5th April, 1958, with the 5.20 pm Penygraig-Llantrisant arriving, a Diagram A27 trailer propelled by 0-4-2T No. 1471.   *Robert Darlaston*

Parcels, but alas no passengers, are unloaded at Tonyrefail, as No. 1471 waits with the 4.55 pm Llantrisant-Penygraig auto-train on 5th April,1958.   *Robert Darlaston*

Tonyrefail station on 24th May, 1958 with No. 1471 about to depart for Llantrisant with the 5.20 pm ex-Penygraig. *Robert Darlaston*

The Penygaig-Llantrisant auto-train stands at the up platform at Tonyrefail on the last day of service, Saturday, 7th June, 1958. *S. Rickard Collection/Copyright B.J. Miller*

A Penygraig-bound auto-train, hauled by No. 1471, runs into the down platform at Tonyrefail on 7th June, 1958.   *John Hodge*

No. 1471 stands at the down platform at Tonyrefail with an auto-train from Llantrisant to Penygraig, 7th June, 1958.   *John Hodge*

slip was added to the crossing north of the station to create a trailing crossover between the up and down running lines. This slip was taken out of use, together with siding connection from the up line, and the signal box closed on 15th January, 1950. The remaining siding connection, to the down line, latterly controlled by a ground frame, was taken out on 5th January, 1964.

Above Tonyrefail station there were, at various times, no less than four colliery sidings within about half a mile. The first of these, Caerlan, on the down side of the line, was controlled by the station signal box. The private siding agreement, dated 29th June, 1915, provided for connections from the up and down main lines. The siding opened on 8th May, 1916, the agreement covering it lasting until about 1936.

Tonyrefail signal box had also controlled the lower junction to Collena Colliery. This colliery was in existence at the opening of the EVR in 1860, with the siding originally taking the form of a simple loop on the up side of the single track main line. Collena saw a number of owners, including Noel Bros. & Co. from 1884, and the Glyn Colliery Co. from 1891, when the colliery sidings were substantially enlarged, to 1903 when it closed. The siding was reopened on 3rd September, 1906 by the Glamorgan Coal Co., but the venture did not prove successful, the siding agreement being terminated on 14th December, 1911.

On 22nd January, 1873 the GWR authorised the construction of a siding to serve the Ely Merthyr Colliery, just above Collena, but on the opposite side of the line. This siding was destined to be very short-lived, however, and had been removed by 1881.

The last of this group of collieries, Cil Ely, had been developed by David Davies, before being let to the GWR in 1874. The siding left the main line just before milepost 5¼, in later years by means of a trailing connection off the up line. On 3rd March, 1875 the GWR authorised the extension of this siding to serve a new shaft which was being sunk at the colliery. The siding agreement passed to Blindell Bros. & Co. in 1896, then to Atlantic Merthyr Collieries Ltd in 1907, Locketts Merthyr Collieries (1894) Ltd. in 1911, and finally to Cil Ely Collieries Ltd in 1934. It was terminated in 1953, following the closure of the colliery in October 1950.

A new signal box, known as 'Cilely Junction' (5 m. 52 ch.), was opened in 1899, on the doubling of the line to this point from Gellyrhaidd Junction. With the extension of the double line through to Penygraig in 1901 the box continued in use, controlling the adjoining colliery sidings, before being closed in 1953.

From Tonyrefail the Ely Valley line had climbed at 1 in 50 to Cilely Junction. When this section was doubled, after 1897, the new down line was constructed at a lower level than the old for about a mile above Cilely Junction, but this still entailed a gradient of 1 in 40 to the summit of the railway near milepost 6¾.

There had been two collieries - Dinas Isaf (or Isha) and Penrhiwfer - near the summit, but these had gone by 1912. Both had opened in the early years of the EVR. On 18th March, 1875, when the GWR authorised the laying of an additional connection to form a loop siding off the main line, Dinas Isaf was in the hands of the Ely Rhondda Colliery. This concern went into liquidation in 1911, with the siding connections being removed in 1913.

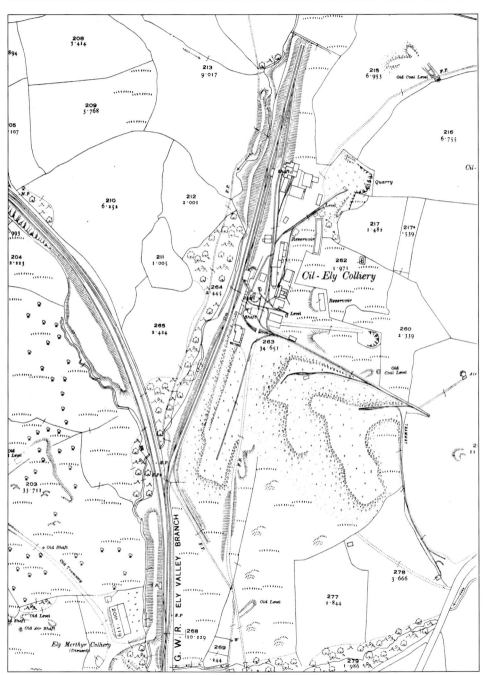

Cil Ely Colliery and the remains of Ely Merthyr Colliery.
Reproduced from the 25″, 1919 Ordnance Survey Map

Penrhiwfer Colliery, on the opposite side of the line, was an even earlier mine, tenders for the construction of the colliery sidings having been sought in February 1863. It was owned by the Glamorgan Coal Co. when on 9th November, 1881 the GWR approved the construction of a second siding connection to the main line. The siding agreement with this company was terminated on 15th November, 1896. These siding connections were controlled, from at least 1889, by Penrhiwfer signal box (6 m. 40 ch.), adjoining the upper junctions to the colliery sidings. In July 1895 a passing loop was authorised at this location, but this decision was quickly overtaken by that to double the line to Penygraig, and it is not clear if this loop was ever completed as such. A new signal box, replacing that at Penrhiwfer and called 'Dinas Isha' (6 m. 35 ch.), was sited between the up and down main lines, and was brought into use with the completion of the doubling in 1901. By this date Penrhiwfer Colliery sidings had gone, leaving the new box to control the connections to Dinas Isaf Colliery, until its closure in 1912.

Just beyond the summit of the line was Naval Sidings signal box (6 m. 64 ch.), which had opened in 1901 in connection with the doubling of the last section of single track through to Penygraig. An agreement had been entered into on 10th August, 1881 with the Naval Steam Coal Co. for a siding to serve Ely Colliery on the down side of the line. This concern was reformed in 1887 and 1897, but retained 'Naval' in its title, before becoming part of the Cambrian Combine in 1908. The siding agreement was terminated on 31st July, 1931, following the closure of the Ely Colliery, the signal box being abandoned not long afterwards, although it was not until 1938 that the siding connection from the up line was removed.

The closure of Ely Colliery did not mean the end of traffic at this place, however, as a further agreement, dated 10th September, 1948, with John Morgan (Builders) Ltd provided for a siding to a tip on the site of the former colliery. This facility had been abandoned by 1950, but on 6th May, 1960 another siding was brought into use nearby to serve an NCB coal stacking site. This proved equally short-lived, the connection being taken out of use on 9th September, 1963.

From Naval Sidings the railway descended at a gradient of 1 in 120 to Penygraig. As extended from Penrhiwfer in 1862, the Ely Valley line had terminated at Dinas goods station, just over 7¼ miles from the junction with the South Wales main line at Llantrisant station. The new terminus had originally comprised two short loop sidings, but on 1st September, 1864 an agreement was entered into for a siding to serve the adjoining colliery of the Penygraig Coal Co. By 1875 large coke ovens had also been installed. This mine later passed to the Naval Co., with the siding agreement terminating on 31st July, 1931.

When the line had opened there was little in the way of habitation at Penygraig, the goods station taking the name 'Dinas' then given to the locality. However, by the end of the 19th century the built-up area extended from Williamstown, below Penygraig, through Tonypandy and on into Clydach Vale.

The Ely & Clydach Valleys Railway had commenced just before the site of the old terminus, near milepost 7. Opened as a single line, a passing loop was authorised at Penygraig on 31st July, 1895, but this was soon incorporated in the doubling of the section above Cilely Junction, completed in 1901. The passenger station (7 m. 22 ch.), opened in May 1901 as 'Penygraig' (the goods station having been renamed in 1885), consisted of separate up and down platforms,

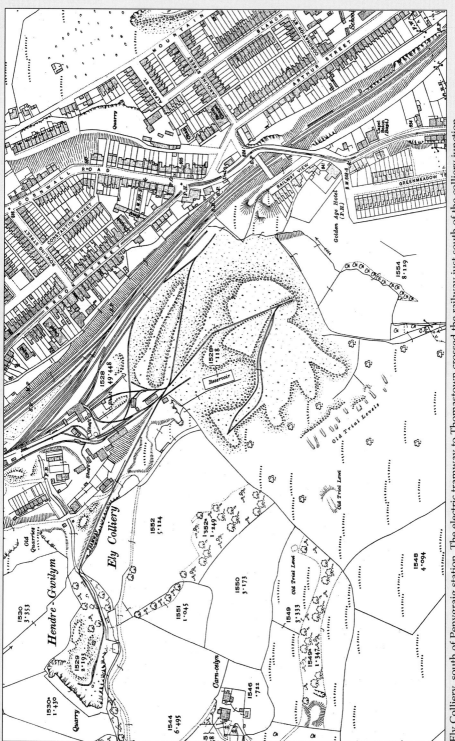

Ely Colliery, south of Penygraig station. The electric tramway to Thomastown crossed the railway just south of the colliery junction.
Reproduced from the 25", 1920 Ordnance Survey Map

A Llantrisant-Penygraig auto-train propelled by No. 1471 climbs towards Penygraig on the last stage of its journey, 7th June, 1958.   The remains of Dinas Isaf Colliery can be seen in the background.   *John Hodge*

A train of empties, hauled by 0-6-0PT No. 3612 and banked by sister engine No. 3644, running past Penygraig yard *en route* to Cambrian Colliery on 20th September, 1962.   *C.H.A. Townley*

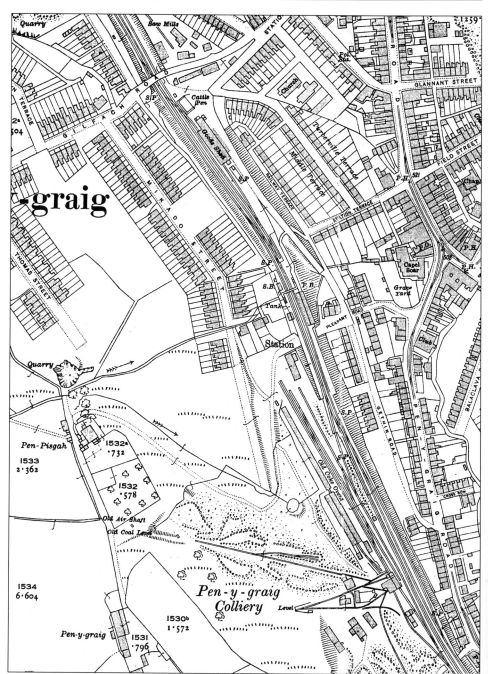

Penygraig Colliery and Penygraig station.   *Reproduced from the 25", 1920 Ordnance Survey Map*

linked by a footbridge. The extensive station building, of timber construction, and complete with a substantial awning, was located on the up platform, with a rather superfluous shelter on the down. Passenger trains, having arrived from Llantrisant at the down platform, normally ran forward, before setting back into the up platform, to await departure.

On 29th June, 1911 the GWR Traffic Committee agreed to change the name of the station to 'Penygraig and Tonypandy', possibly in recognition of the competition provided by the TVR's Tonypandy and Trealaw station, opened in 1908. The renaming took effect on 12th July, 1911, but was not to last, the station reverting to the more accurate title of 'Penygraig' on 13th July, 1925. A substantial improvement to the booking hall accommodation, at an estimated cost of £397, was approved by the Traffic Committee on 30th January, 1913. The station buildings were removed in the early 1950s, being replaced by a rather undistinguished single-storey building providing somewhat limited shelter and booking facilities.

Penygraig signal box was originally sited alongside the up line, just south of the platform, but, on 1st June, 1911, it was replaced by a new box (7 m. 25 ch.) on the down platform, near its northern end. This box was closed on 9th September, 1963, on the singling of the line above Gellyrhaidd Junction.

At first the new goods station, opened in 1878, took its name from the old, but on 25th March, 1885 it was agreed that it be changed to 'Penygraig', the renaming being effective from 1st April of that year. It was situated just beyond the passenger station on the up side of the line. On 13th August, 1891 the GWR authorised the laying of additional sidings, together with the extension of the goods shed, with the tender of A. Woodhouse for the latter being accepted on 7th April, 1892 for the sum of £1,795. New cattle pens were authorised on 20th April, 1904, with approval for a goods platform following on 6th May, 1908. The track layout in the yard was drastically reduced at the time of the singling of the line in 1963. By the time of its closure in October 1964 it consisted of just one siding off the running line, the private siding agreement for the adjoining timber yard having been terminated on 1st January, 1961.

Just beyond the goods yard, but on the opposite side of the line, was Nantgwyn Colliery. A connection off the single line had been authorised by the GWR on 13th August, 1891, with the private siding agreement with the Naval Colliery Co. being entered into on 7th April, 1892. The doubling of the line completed in 1901 included the provision of a second line of rails from Penygraig station to Nantgwyn North ground frame (8 m. 01 ch.). However, above Nantgwyn South ground frame (7 m. 43 ch.), the point at which normal double line working commenced, this second line took the form of a down siding. This was made 'dead end' and cut back at its northern extremity in July 1959. The agreement for Nantgwyn siding was terminated on 31st July, 1931, following the abandonment of the colliery. A siding was later opened to a tip for John Morgan (Builders) Ltd on the site of Nantgwyn Colliery under an agreement dated 10th September, 1948, but this agreement came to an end on 28th July, 1963.

Above Nantgwyn the line curved along the hillside towards its terminus at Clydach Vale, the gradient rising rapidly from 1 in 220 to a fearsome 1 in 32. Just over ½ mile after Nantgwyn North was a loop siding serving Nant Rhondda Colliery. This had been brought into use on 26th April, 1914, under an

No. 1471 and its crew at Penygraig prior to working
the 5.20 pm to Llantrisant on 24th May, 1958.
Robert Darlaston

Penygraig signal box is shown to advantage in this view of the station
and Ely Valley auto-train on 7th June, 1958.   *John Hodge*

A pair of 0-6-0PTs and brake vans, with leading engine No.4637 taking water at the up platform at Penygraig on 15th February, 1958. *Hugh Davies*

A wet winter's day at Penygraig with 0-6-0PT No. 3612 just arrived on a passenger working from Llantrisant, 15th February, 1958. *S. Rickard Collection/Copyright B.J. Miller*

No. 1471 sets its Diagram A27 auto-trailer back into the up platform at Penygraig prior to departure for Llantrisant, *c*. 1958.   *Hugh Davies*

Penygraig, looking towards the goods yard on 24th May, 1958. No. 1471 is shunting its auto-trailer across from the down line into the up platform to await departure for Llantrisant.
                                                                            Robert Darlaston

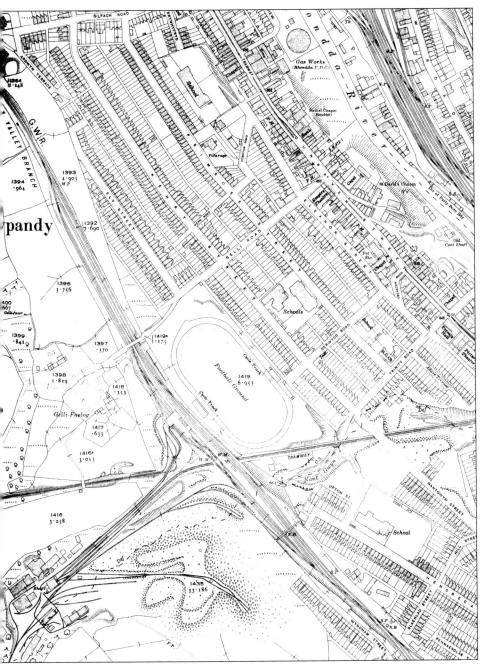

Nantgwyn Colliery (*bottom left*), to the north of Penygraig station. Just visible (*top right*) is the
TVR's Rhondda Fawr branch.   *Reproduced from the 25", 1920 Ordnance Survey Map*

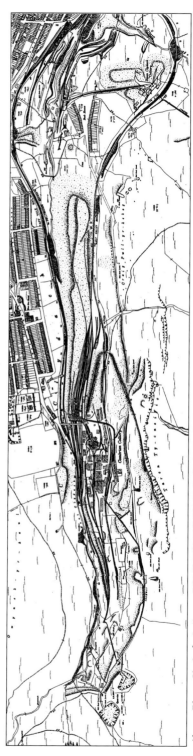

Above: Blaen Clydach Colliery to Cambrian Colliery and the end of the line. The TVR line to Cambrian Colliery can be seen to the north of the EVR.
Reproduced from the 25", 1919 Ordnance Survey Map

Right: 0-6-0PT No. 3612 at the end of the line at Clydach Vale, ready to set empties back under the screens at Cambrian Colliery, while an NCB locomotive stands alongside, 20th September, 1962.
C.H.A. Townley

agreement with the Rhondda House Coal Co., but this concern soon changed its name to the 'Nant Rhondda Colliery Co.'. This company went into liquidation about 1935, but the siding agreement was not terminated until 31st December, 1945, the connection itself being removed during the following year.

The Cambrian Colliery at Clydach Vale, just over 9 miles from Llantrisant, had been the principal objective of the E&CVR, and was to provide a rich reward for the railway over the years. As we have seen, the original siding had been approved by the GWR in 1882, with second connection to the colliery sidings being installed under an agreement of 6th August, 1897. The junctions were controlled by a cabin at 9 m. 03 ch., but in 1921 this was replaced by a new signal box called 'Clydach Vale', midway between the two sidings. This box was closed on 3rd October, 1965. Cambrian Colliery was the scene of two major disasters, the first on 10th March, 1905, when 31 miners lost their lives, and the second on 17th May, 1965, resulting in an identical number of deaths. The private siding agreement came to an end on 31st March, 1967.

The railway continued beyond the colliery sidings into the upper reaches of Cwm Clydach. On 9th October, 1889 the GWR gave permission for Thomas, Riches & Co. to use a portion of the line 'over which traffic is not at present worked' to bring coal out from their new pit to their sidings, the colliery company paying the cost (£40) of putting the line in good order.

Clydach Vale colliers' platform (9 m. 23 ch.) was situated on this section, just beyond the upper colliery junction. Provided under an agreement (dated 5th May, 1899) with the colliery company, this platform was reached by a short loop off the running line. Under a further agreement of 8th December, 1920, it was proposed to resite the platform at the entrance to the colliery sidings, but this scheme was subsequently abandoned. The original platform agreement was terminated on 19th May, 1931, the workmen's trains having ceased to run by 1926.

In June 1938 the line above 9 m. 06 ch. was acquired by Powell Duffryn Associated Collieries Ltd, the GWR having obtained powers for the abandonment of this section under its Act of 10th June, 1937.

A '57XX' 0-6-0PT stands at the rear of a train of empties at Clydach Vale on 24th May, 1960. *F.A. Blencoe*

An 0-6-0PT shunts at the Cambrian Colliery, Clydach Vale, in severe winter conditions c. 1963.

R. Mason

The Mwyndy Branch

From Mwyndy Junction there was a short length of double track, past Cowbridge Road Crossing signal box (0 m. 16 ch.), which had opened in 1901. An attractive single-storey crossing keeper's lodge, reminiscent of a toll gate house, had existed at Cowbridge Road, but this was lost to road widening in the early 1930s. The signal box was reduced to the status of a ground frame on 3rd October, 1965, when the line from Mwyndy Junction was singled. On 3rd February, 1974 the crossing gates were replaced by lifting barriers, which, from 10th October, 1983, were operated by the train crew. The former signal box was then taken out of use and subsequently demolished.

The single line commenced just beyond Cowbridge Road Crossing (0 m. 22 ch.). New Park siding ground frame (0 m. 31 ch.), on the down side of the line just beyond this point, controlled a private siding brought into use in 1943 to serve a Ministry of Food storage depot. This siding was taken out of use on 9th May, 1966. The Mwyndy branch then ran dead straight and due east to Maesaraul Junction. About halfway along this section there had been, in the early days, a siding serving a small colliery to the south of the line, the *Cardiff Times* of 12th February, 1864 reporting that 'On Tuesday (9th February) the Hendy Mining Co. succeeded in winning the Rock Vein Coal in their New Park Pit'.

At Maesaraul Junction the ex-TVR line to Treforest left the Mwyndy branch, although the site of the junction itself moved about a bit over the years. Its

The 11.0 am Llantrisant-Pontypridd Coke Ovens Sidings mixed freight, hauled by class '56XX' 0-6-2T No. 5618 and banked by 0-6-0PT No. 3617, approaches Cowbridge Road Crossing on the short double track section from Mwyndy Junction on 3rd May, 1958.
S. Rickard Collection/Copyright B.J. Miller

An early view of Cowbridge Road Crossing signal box showing the single storey gate-keepers lodge alongside.   *Welsh Industrial & Maritime Museum*

Cowbridge Road Crossing signal box on 30th April, 1972 with gas lamps and level crossing gates still intact.   *J.A. Sommerfield*

Cowbridge Road Crossing signal box in the days of single track and lifting barriers, 10th May, 1982.
R.W. Ranson

The Mwyndy branch goods, hauled by 0-6-0PT No.4674 and bearing target number H81, passes Maesaraul Junction ground frame on 10th September, 1960. The train is conveying a wagon of coal for Bevans at Maesaraul Siding and two gunpowder vans for the ICI depot at Mwyndy.
E.V. Richards

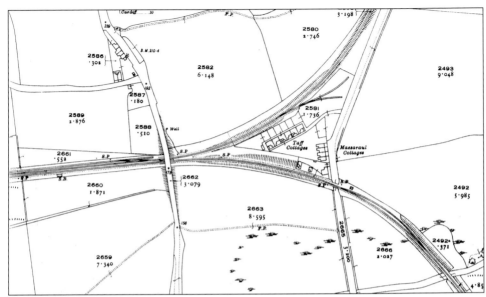

Maesaraul Junction and Maesaraul Siding on the Mwyndy branch. Just north of Taff Cottages is Cottage Siding on the former L&TVJR line. *Reproduced from the 25", 1919 Ordnance Survey Map*

Pannier tank No. 9780 with the Mwyndy branch goods (target 'Z8') at Maesaraul Crossing on 15th August, 1957. The gatekeeper's lodge was similar in style to that which had once existed at Cowbridge Road Crossing.   *Ian L. Wright*

The Mwyndy branch goods, hauled by 0-6-0PT No. 9780, passes Maesaraul Crossing on its return to Llantrisant on 15th August, 1957. *Ian L. Wright*

original position at the actual divergence of the two lines having falling foul of the Board of Trade in 1863, the junction was relocated just under a quarter of a mile to the west. Minor alterations were carried out in 1884 and again in 1906, but in January 1930 it was moved back to more or less its original site (1 m. 02 ch.). A further move eastwards, this time by only by 2 chains, was completed on 20th May, 1945. The first signal box had been situated at the junction itself, but was replaced in 1884 by a new box, about 6 chains to the east of the actual junction. This was replaced by a covered ground frame in January 1930.

Beyond the junction the Mwyndy branch curved to the south, over Maesaraul Crossing and past Maesaraul Siding. This short loop siding, which had been authorised by the EVR Board on 23rd August, 1860, was latterly used by a local coal merchant and taken out of use on 1st February, 1965.

About 1½ miles from Mwyndy Junction the branch reached the site of its first iron ore mine, served by Bute Siding on the up side of the line. Extensive sidings had existed here, with the quarries being linked to the railway by a complex system of tramways. Although the Bute iron ore mine was closed in 1881, the siding retained its original name and lasted, albeit in a much reduced form, for many years. Limestone rather than iron ore was the staple traffic, with a tramway connecting the siding to a quarry near Miskin. The siding passed through a number of users, before the last agreement was terminated on 17th February, 1966.

On the opposite side of the line a short loop siding serving an ICI explosives depot. The termination of the siding agreement on 2nd September, 1968 was followed by the closure of the branch beyond Maesaraul Junction later that year.

R. *Mason*

The Mwyndy branch goods, hauled by 0-6-0PT No. 3644, at Maesaraul Siding *c.* 1963.

0-6-0PT No. 3644 at Bute Siding on the Mwyndy branch, with the ICI explosives depot on the right, c. 1963. R. Mason

From Bute Siding the line curved through a broad arc to run in an easterly direction, past the site of the Mwyndy iron ore mine. Mwyndy Siding had cut across this arc from its junction (1 m. 55 ch.), to rejoin the Mwyndy branch further on (2 m. 12 ch.). Tramways connected this loop line with the iron ore workings to the north. After the closure of the iron ore mine in 1884, the loop line was cut back to form a short dead-end siding, known as 'Scull's Siding', at the eastern end. Around the turn of the century an unsuccessful attempt was made to re-open the Mwyndy iron ore mine, with a private siding agreement being entered into with the Llantrisant Ochre Oxide Iron Ore Syndicate on 30th August, 1899. The re-instated Mwyndy Siding passed to R.E. Morgan in 1903, and in 1928 it was listed as serving sawmills belonging to Williams & Sons of Llantrisant. The siding agreement was eventually terminated on 18th July, 1966.

With the removal of the last mile of track to Brofiscin in 1936, the Mwyndy branch was cut back to a point (1 m. 63 ch.) just east of the junction with Mwyndy Siding.

Beyond Scull's Siding there had been two more sidings serving iron ore workings: Llwynsaer (2 m. 24 ch.) and Dowlais (near milepost 2½), the former having closed in 1881 and the latter before that date. On 7th February, 1883 the GWR authorised the re-laying of Llwynsaer Siding for the Mwyndy Iron Ore Co. This re-opening was not a success, however, and the siding agreement came to an end on 30th November, 1891, the siding itself being removed the following January.

The end of the line at Mwyndy *c.* 1963. The section of the branch from here to Brofiscin was removed in November 1936.   *R. Mason*

The Mwyndy branch goods prepares to depart from the terminus with a single gunpowder van and brake van, the latter conveying a number of passengers on this occasion, *c.* 1963.   *R. Mason*

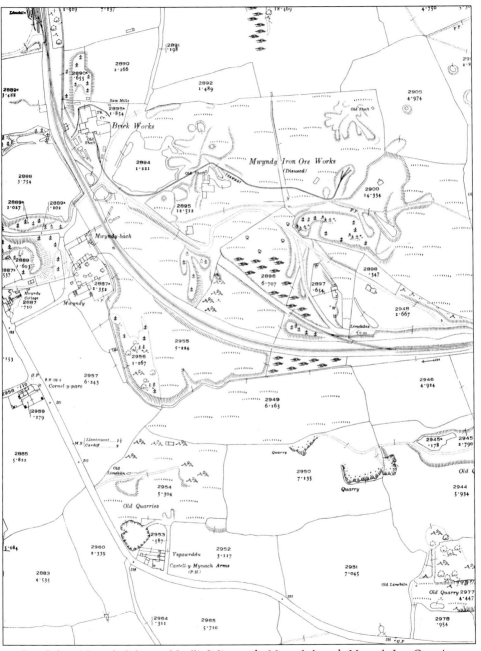

Bute Siding, Mwyndy Siding and Scull's Siding on the Mwyndy branch. Mwyndy Iron Ore mine had been served off a loop line between the last two sidings.

Reproduced from the 25", 1919 Ordnance Survey Map

The terminus of the Mwyndy branch (2 m. 63 ch.) at Brofiscin took the form of an end-on junction with a very short private siding, latterly used by J.H. Morgan and serving a limeworks from where a tramway ran to a quarry to the south of the line.

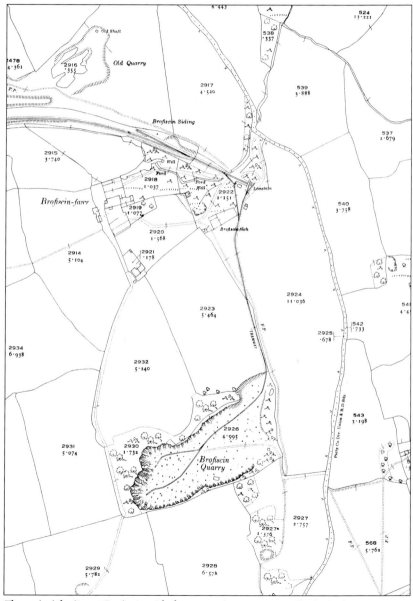

The end of the line at Brofiscin with the connecting tramway to Brofiscin Quarry.
Reproduced from the 25", 1919 Ordnance Survey Map

The Castellau Branch

As has been seen, this branch closed in 1867, having only ever been broad gauge. It left the main line of the EVR at milepost 1¾ before curving away to the north-east and bridging the River Ely. It then passed on a low embankment through the fields to Glanmychydd Fawr, from where it ran alongside a stream known as the Nant Mychydd. Shortly before its terminus near Glanmychydd Fach, a spur line went off to the east, to terminate near the site of the later Treferig Junction. On 2nd October, 1857 the EVR Board gave instructions concerning land for a 'station' at the terminus of the Castellau branch, but nothing else is known. When the Treferig Valley Railway opened in 1883 a short spur line was provided to the site of the terminus of the Castellau branch. On 28th August, 1879 a letter from the Treferig promoters was read at the GWR Board, informing the Directors that work on the new railway was about to start, and asking the company to relay the Castellau branch, but nothing came of this request.

The Gellyrhaidd Branch

It is not clear what if any traffic was worked over the Gellyrhaidd branch prior to the opening of the Ely Valley Extension Railway in 1865. On 19th August, 1874 the GWR authorised the construction of two junctions to serve a colliery siding, for a Mr Humby, but the location of this siding (if in fact it was provided) has not been identified.

When the main line through Gellyrhaidd Junction was doubled in 1899, a short section of double line was also provided on the Gellyrhaidd branch, the single line then commencing just before the bridge carrying the branch over the River Ely (0 m. 15 ch.)

A short distance beyond this bridge there had been a loop siding, authorised by the GWR on 30th July, 1890, serving the Ely Llantwit Colliery. This siding was controlled by two ground frames (0 m. 17 ch. and 0 m. 30 ch.), but did not last long, being removed shortly after the termination of the siding agreement on 30th April, 1898.

By 1913 facilities at Tonyrefail goods yard were becoming increasingly congested, without any scope for improvement. In order to give some relief, the GWR Traffic Commitee agreed, on 19th January, 1913, to provide additional accommodation on the site of the former Ely Llantwit Colliery, the new facility, known as 'Gellyrhaidd (or 'Thomastown') Mileage Siding' opening on 20th April, 1914.

Another loop siding (1 m. 21 ch. and 1 m. 36 ch.) had also existed on the Gellyrhaidd branch, serving the Welsh Wallsend Colliery, having been laid in during March 1881 and removed on 20th May, 1885. A later siding at this place was used by the Gellyrhaidd Colliery.

The Gellyrhaidd branch made an end-on connection with the EVER just before Hendreforgan station (1 m. 55 ch.). The station itself consisted of a single platform with run-round loop, and a short goods siding to the rear of the platform. There were also a number of loop and dead-end sidings for the coal traffic. Immediately to the west of the platform was the junction of the branch to Gilfach Goch with the line to Blackmill.

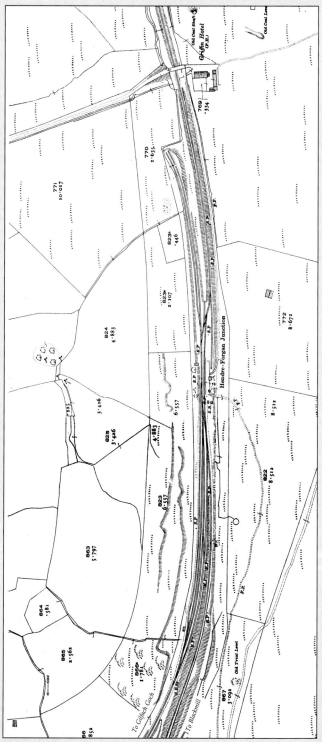

Hendreforgan station, to the west of the end-on junction between the Gellyrhaidd branch and the former Ely Valley Extension Railway.

Reproduced from the 25", 1919 Ordnance Survey Map

Chapter Ten

Postscript

After the removal of the track above Coed Ely in August 1967 the earthworks and other remains of this part of the Ely Valley line took on an increasingly derelict appearance. However, in the congested valleys of South Wales former transport routes such as this are not discarded lightly. Most of the old line above Coed Ely has since been incorporated in a new road through the upper reaches of the Ely Valley and on into that of the Rhondda Fawr, the whole forming an extension of the earlier Ely Valley Road. The first section of this new road, between Coed Ely and Williamstown, was opened on 20th January, 1986, providing a much-needed by-pass for Tonyrefail. The continuation above Williamstown opened as the rather prosaically titled 'Mid-Rhondda Access Road' on 5th October, 1988. This took in the remainder of this northern section of the former EVR, together with part of the ex-E&CVR route, as far as Tonypandy. From there use was made of the remains of the Pwllyrhebog Incline to reach the main road running along the floor of the Rhondda Fawr Valley. About a mile of the former Gellyrhaidd branch was subsequently used to provide a link road to the Tonyrefail bypass.

Part of the Mwyndy branch has also been used as a route for a new road, in this case the Talbot Green By-pass, which was opened on 1st November, 1991. Here, however, the railway itself was not lost, but was realigned to the north of the new road under powers contained in the British Railways Act 1987. The new section of railway, which included a level crossing over the new by-pass, was completed in March 1993, although, at the time of writing, the hoped-for return of traffic to the Coke Ovens at Cwm has yet to materialise. A railtour, the 'Gwaun-Cae-Gurwen Growler II', organised by the Monmouthshire Railway Society, ran over the branch as far as the new level crossing on 23rd April, 1994.

After nearly 30 years, Llantrisant station was reborn as 'Pontyclun', with the new station opening on the site of the old on 28th September, 1992, on the re-introduction of local passenger trains between Cardiff, Bridgend and Maesteg. A 'feeder' bus service between Pontyclun station and Tonyrefail was not a success, however, and was soon withdrawn.

Thus the wheel has all but turned full circle, with the railway system throughout the length of the Ely Valley having receded to that which existed when the Prospectus for the EVR was published in 1856, apart from the section of the former Mwyndy branch from Llantrisant Yard to the site of Maesaraul Junction, which forms part of the extant but unused Cwm branch. However, coal traffic may yet return to this line. In its Network Management Statement of March 2000 Railtrack confirmed that it was evaluating the re-opening of the branch to serve Cwm Coking Works.

The junction with the Ely Valley line and the site of Llantrisant station viewed from the bridge over the South Wales main line on 8th June, 1983. *Robert Darlaston*

The new station at Pontyclun looking towards Bridgend in 1995. The facing crossover and trailing connection off the up line provide access to Llantrisant yard. *Bill John*

Sources and Bibliography

Research for this book has relied to a very large extent on primary sources and contemporary journals. Much has come from the Public Record Office at Kew, including material from EVR, GWR and other companies' minute books and reports, and Board of Trade inspection reports and other documents. Leicester University has provided a convenient source for Private and Local Acts, Parliamentary Notices in the *London Gazette*, British Railways, GWR and *Bradshaw's* timetables, and journals such as the *Railway Times*, *Railway News*, the *Railway Engineer*, and the *Great Western Railway Magazine*. Contemporary newspapers were mainly consulted at Cardiff Central Library, and included the *Cardiff & Merthyr Guardian*, the *Cardiff Times* and the *Western Mail*. For more recent events the *Railway Observer* proved most helpful.

Books and articles consulted included:

Barry Docks and Railways Vol. 1, I.W. Prothero, 1995
Barry - The Centenary Book, Ed. D. Moore, Barry, 1984
British Trolleybus Systems: Rhondda in *Buses*, A.G. Newman and C.J. Taylor, 1982
Cardiff and the Marquesses of Bute, J. Davies, University of Wales Press, 1981
Coal Mining in and around Llantrisant, T. Boyns, paper delivered to the Llantrisant and District Local History Society, 1983
The Cowbridge Railway, C. Chapman, Oxford Publishing Co., 1984
Great Western Auto Trailers, J. Lewis, Wild Swan, 1991
History of the Great Western Railway, E.T. MacDermot, GWR, 1927
History of Port of Cardiff, E.L. Chappell, The Priory Press Ltd, 1939
The Llantrisant Branches of the TVR, C. Chapman, Oakwood Press, 1996
The Locomotives of the GWR, The Railway Correspondence and Travel Society
The Rhondda Transport Company Limited, Public Service Vehicle Circle / Omnibus Society, 1967
The Rhondda Valleys, E.D. Lewis, University College Cardiff Press, 1958
The South Wales Coal Industry 1841-1875, J.H. Morris and L.J. Williams, 1958

Acknowledgements

Railway research thrives in an open and friendly environment and so I would like to acknowledge the contribution of all those who have helped with the preparation of this book. Special mention should be made of Graham Croad, both for the benefit of his local knowledge and for taking the time and trouble to plough through local council minute books looking for and finding much of railway interest. Thanks are also due to Derek Chaplin, Tony Cooke, Robert Darlaston, John Dore Dennis, Dr Charles Donovan, Michael Hale, Cliff Harris, John Hodge, Bill John, Bob Marrows, Brian Miller, Tony Miller, Jim Peden, Rowland Pittard, the late Iorwerth Prothero, R.W. Ranson, Dick Riley, Chris Taylor, Bryan Wilson, Ian Wright and many other members of the Welsh Railways Research Circle, Historical Model Railway Society and the Railway & Canal Historical Society, too numerous to mention. Thanks must also go to my wife Diana, for her continuing patience and understanding.

Index